lonely planet

Pocket
İSTANBUL
TOP SIGHTS • LOCAL LIFE • MADE EASY

Virginia Maxwell

In This Book

QuickStart Guide

Your keys to understanding the city – we help you decide what to do and how to do it

Need to Know
Tips for a smooth trip

Neighbourhoods
What's where

Explore İstanbul

The best things to see and do, neighbourhood by neighbourhood

Top Sights
Make the most of your visit

Local Life
The insider's city

The Best of İstanbul

The city's highlights in handy lists to help you plan

Best Walks
See the city on foot

İstanbul's Best...
The best experiences

Survival Guide

Tips and tricks for a seamless, hassle-free city experience

Getting Around
Travel like a local

Essential Information
Including where to stay

Our selection of the city's best places to eat, drink and experience:

⊙ **Sights**

⊗ **Eating**

🍷 **Drinking**

✪ **Entertainment**

🔒 **Shopping**

···

These symbols give you the vital information for each listing:

🎜	Telephone Numbers	👪	Family-Friendly
⏱	Opening Hours	🐾	Pet-Friendly
P	Parking	🚌	Bus
🚭	Nonsmoking	🛳	Ferry
@	Internet Access	M	Metro
🛜	Wi-Fi Access	🚋	Tram
🥗	Vegetarian Selection	🚆	Train
📖	English-Language Menu		

···

Find each listing quickly on maps for each neighbourhood:

Bar Hemingway

16 🍷 Map p233, B2

Legend has it that Hemi self, wielding a machine ...rate this timber-pan ...ered bar during ... showpiece is a ...en by Papa a ...town. Dress ...s.com; Hôtel Rit ...⏱6.30pm-2a

Lonely Planet's İstanbul

Lonely Planet Pocket Guides are designed to get you straight to the heart of the city.

Inside you'll find all the must-see sights, plus tips to make your visit to each one really memorable. We've split the city into easy-to-navigate neighbourhoods and provided clear maps so you'll find your way around with ease. Our expert writers have searched out the best of the city: walks, food, nightlife and shopping, to name a few. Because you want to explore, our 'Local Life' pages will take you to some of the most exciting areas to experience the real İstanbul.

And of course you'll find all the practical tips you need for a smooth trip: itineraries for short visits, how to get around, and how much to tip the guy who serves you a drink at the end of a long day's exploration.

It's your guarantee of a really great experience.

Our Promise

You can trust our travel information because Lonely Planet authors visit the places we write about, each and every edition. We never accept freebies for positive coverage, so you can rely on us to tell it like it is.

QuickStart Guide 7

Explore İstanbul 21

Worth a Trip:

The Best of İstanbul 119

İstanbul's Best Walks

İstanbul's Best...

Survival Guide 143

QuickStart Guide

Welcome to İstanbul

In İstanbul, extraordinary experiences are found around every corner. Here, dervishes whirl, *müezzins* call from minarets and people move between continents multiple times a day. Home to millennia-old monuments and cutting-edge art galleries (sometimes in the same block), it's a destination where eating, drinking and dancing are local priorities, and where everyone is welcome to join the party.

Sema (whirling-dervish ceremony)
RESUL MUSLU/SHUTTERSTOCK ©

İstanbul Top Sights

Aya Sofya (p24)

History resonates when you visit this majestic basilica. Built in the 6th century AD, its remarkable features include a massive dome and a stunning collection of Byzantine mosaics.

Topkapı Palace
(p44)

The sultans lived in this pavilion-style palace with their families, concubines and servants during the glory days of the Ottoman Empire. Reminders of their privileged lifestyles are everywhere to be seen.

The Bosphorus
(p114)

A ferry trip down the mighty Bosphorus Strait showcases a passing parade of mosques, palaces and mansions on both the Asian and European shores.

Grand Bazaar (p60)

Sometimes described as the world's oldest and most evocative shopping mall, this colourful and chaotic covered market is the heart of İstanbul's Old City and one of its most atmospheric attractions.

Süleymaniye Mosque (p64)

Truly deserving the tag 'living history', this imperial mosque atop the city's fourth hill is one of the few that has retained, restored and creatively reused its original outbuildings.

İstanbul Archaeology Museums (p48)

An eclectic and exhilarating collection of antiquities, classical sculpture, Ottoman tilework and Byzantine artefacts is showcased at this museum complex next to Topkapı Palace.

Kariye Museum
(Chora Church; p80)

Great things can come in small packages. This diminutive Byzantine church is made extraordinary by virtue of its interior, which is adorned with exquisite mosaics and frescoes.

İstiklal Caddesi (p84)

A promenade down this pedestrianised 19th-century boulevard is the quintessential İstanbul experience, offering a colourful snapshot of local life.

Pera Museum (p86)

Staging temporary exhibitions, including this work by Ania Soliman (http://aniasoliman.com; pictured), alongside its magnificent permanent collection of Orientalist works, this museum is a must-see.

Blue Mosque (p28)

Beloved of tourists and locals alike, the most photogenic of İstanbul's imperial mosques is also one of the busiest places of worship in the city.

JESSIE DUROCHER/GETTY IMAGES ©

OZGUR GUVENC/SHUTTERSTOCK ©

Basilica Cistern (p30)

Both architectural tour de force and virtuosic engineering feat, this evocatively lit underground cistern is one of İstanbul's most mysterious and magnificent Byzantine monuments.

Dolmabahçe Palace (p106)

This palace on the Bosphorus shore – built as the Ottoman Empire's power waned but making no concessions to this fact – offers an intriguing look at the artificial lives and ostentatious taste of the rulers.

İstanbul Local Life

Insider tips to help you find the real city

İstanbul's 14 million residents enjoy an exhilarating lifestyle that is crammed with culture, enriched by history and underpinned by family and faith. Head to their neighbourhoods, mosques, shops and cafes to see what makes life here so special.

Between the Bazaars (p66)

▸ Local shopping
▸ Historic buildings

The winding streets linking the historic Grand and Spice Bazaars are crammed with İstanbullus every day of the week except Sunday. Locals have purchased provisions, outfitted themselves and stocked up on household goods of every possible description here for centuries, and most show no sign of moving their custom to the soulless shopping malls found in the suburbs. Celebrate this fact by punctuating your visit to İstanbul with some exploration of the bazaars.

Cihangir & Çukurcuma (p88)

▸ Ottoman houses
▸ Cafe culture

Though only a short distance away from action-packed İstiklal Caddesi, these two residential districts are relatively quiet and resolutely local. The steep and winding streets are lined with pretty timber houses and elegant apartment blocks dating from the 19th century, interspersed with bohemian cafes, neighbourhood *bakkals* (grocery shops) and junk stores in which the occasional antique treasure can be unearthed.

Weekend Wander in Ortaköy (p108)

▸ Snack and market stalls
▸ Bosphorus views

A former fishing village, Ortaköy makes the most of its magnificent Bosphorus location. Centred on a waterside square full of eateries and cafes, the suburb is home to one of the city's prettiest mosques and plays host to crowds of locals on weekends, who flock here to promenade, take ferry cruises, snack on local fast foods, browse the stalls of the Sunday handicrafts market and drink in the bars and cafes.

Waterfront and mosque at Ortaköy

Antique store in Çukurcuma

Other great places to experience the city like a local:

Küçük Ayasofya (p40)

Hocapaşa Sokak (p56)

Women's Bazaar (p71)

Eminönü fish sandwich stands (p74)

Mimar Sinan Teras Cafe (p76)

Manda Batmaz (p98)

İstanbul Day Planner

Day One

Head to Aya Sofya Meydanı and work out which of the museums and mosques in the immediate area will be on your visiting list. Don't miss **Aya Sofya** (p24), the **Blue Mosque** (p28) and the **Basilica Cistern** (p30). After your visits, wander through the **Hippodrome** (p33), where chariot races were held in ancient times.

Spend the afternoon admiring the huge collection of classical, Byzantine and Ottoman artefacts in the **İstanbul Archaeology Museums** (p48), or the exquisite carpets and calligraphy in the **Museum of Turkish & Islamic Arts** (p33).

After dinner, claim a table at **Derviş Aile Çay Bahçesi** (p38) or **Cafe Meşale** (p39), where you can enjoy tea and a nargile (water pipe). Alternatively, head to the **A'YA Rooftop Lounge** (p39) at the ritzy Four Seasons Hotel at Sultanahmet to admire its panoramic view. In winter a treatment at one of the Old City's **Ottoman-era hamams** (p132) is a relaxing and warm alternative.

Day Two

It's time to investigate the lifestyles of the sultans at **Topkapı Palace** (p44). You'll need a half-day to explore the palace Harem, marvel at the precious objects in the Treasury, admire the recently renovated palace kitchens and wander through the pavilion-filled grounds.

Cross the Galata Bridge to explore the streets, cafes and boutiques of Galata, Tophane, Karaköy and Çukurcuma and consider a visit to the cutting-edge **ARTER** (p85) and **İstanbul Modern** (p92) galleries, the eclectic **Pera Museum** (p86) or the nostalgic **Museum of Innocence** (p92).

The night is still young! Hit the bars and clubs in Asmalımescit, on **İstiklal Caddesi** (p97) or in **Cihangir** (p88). Those who are still hungry should instead head to Karaköy for a late-night baklava fix at **Karaköy Güllüoğlu** (p95).

Short on time?
We've arranged İstanbul's must-sees into these day-by-day itineraries to make sure you see the very best of the city in the time you have available.

Day Three

☼ Get ready to explore the city's famous Bazaar District. After visiting the magnificent **Süleymaniye Mosque** (p64), make your way to the **Grand Bazaar** (p60) to explore its labyrinthine lanes and hidden caravanserais, picking up a few souvenirs along the way.

☼ After enjoying lunch at one of the bazaar district's many cheap eateries, follow the steady stream of local shoppers making their way down the hill to the streets around the **Spice Bazaar** (p70). While there, seek out the exquisite, tile-adorned **Rüstem Paşa Mosque** (p67) and **Hünkâr Kasrı** (p70). As the sun starts to set, head towards **Galata Tower** (p93) and the eating and entertainment district of Beyoğlu.

★ After dinner, listen to some live jazz at **Nardis Jazz Club** (p100) or **Salon** (p100). Alternatively, take a taxi to **Babylon Bomonti** (p139), the city's best-known live-music venue.

Day Four

☼ Board the Long Bosphorus Tour (Uzun Boğaz Turu) with **İstanbul Şehir Hatları** (p148) for a one-way trip up the **Bosphorus** (p114) and then make your way back to town by bus, visiting museums and monuments along the way. Alternatively, take the **Dentur Avraysa** (p148) hop-on, hop-off tour from Beşiktaş and visit the **Sakıp Sabancı Museum** (p116) in Emirgan and the Ottoman-era **Küçüksu Kasrı** (p116) and **Beylerbeyi Palace** (p115).

☼ If you decided to take a 90-minute cruise on a Bosphorus excursion boat rather than the full-day or hop-on, hop-off trip, you can devote the afternoon to visiting the **Kariye Museum** (Chora Church; p80) or **Dolmabahçe Palace** (p106).

★ Bid farewell to the city over a post-dinner drink at one of Beyoğlu's **rooftop bars** (p97) or make your way to **Akarsu Yokuşu** (p88) in Cihangir to wind down in one of its bohemian cafes.

Need to Know

For more information, see Survival Guide (p143)

Currency
Türk Lirası (Turkish lira; ₺)

Language
Turkish

Visas
Not required for some (predominantly European) nationalities; most other nationalities can obtain a 90-day visa electronically at www.evisa.gov.tr.

Money
ATMs are widespread. Credit cards accepted at most shops, hotels and upmarket restaurants.

Mobile Phone
Most European and Australasian phones work here; some North American phones don't. Check with your provider. Prepaid SIM cards must be registered when purchased.

Time
Eastern European Time (UTC/GMT plus three hours). Note: the Turkish government decided in September 2016 to retain daylight-saving (summer) time year-round.

Tipping
A tip of 10% is usual in most restaurants. Round taxi fares up to the nearest lira.

 **Before You Go**

Your Daily Budget

Budget: Less than €60
▶ Dorm bed: €10–25
▶ Kebap or pide dinner: €6
▶ Beer at a neighbourhood bar: €5

Midrange: €60–200
▶ Double room: from €90
▶ *Lokanta* (eatery serving ready-made food) lunch: €8
▶ *Meyhane* (tavern) dinner with wine: €25

Top End: More than €200
▶ Double room: from €200
▶ Restaurant dinner with wine: €35
▶ Cocktail in a rooftop bar: €12

Useful Websites

Canım İstanbul (http://canimistanbul.com/blog/en) Lifestyle-focused blog that's heavy on listings and events.

İstanbul Eats (http://istanbuleats.com) Fab foodie blog.

Lonely Planet (www.lonelyplanet.com/istanbul) Destination information, hotel bookings, traveller forum and more.

Yabangee (www.yabangee.com) Expats' guide to the city, with loads of events listings.

Advance Planning

Three months before If you're travelling in spring, autumn or Christmas, make your hotel booking as far in advance as possible.

Two months before İstanbul's big-ticket festivals and concerts sell out fast. Book your tickets online at **Biletix** (📞 0216-556 9800; www.biletix.com).

Two weeks before Ask your hotel to make dinner reservations.

Arriving in İstanbul

Two international airports currently service the city: **Atatürk International Airport** (IST, Atatürk Havalimanı; ☏+90 444 9828; www.ataturkairport.com) and **Sabiha Gökçen International Airport** (SAW, Sabiha Gökçen Havalimanı; ☏0216-588 8888; www.sgairport.com). At the time of research there were no international rail connections, but this situation may change when upgrades to rail lines throughout the country are completed and the security situation in the region improves.

✈ From Atatürk International Airport

Destination	Best Transport
Old City (including Sultanahmet)	Metro & tram
Beyoğlu	Metro or Havataş airport bus
Bosphorus suburbs	Taxi

✈ From Sabiha Gökçen International Airport

Destination	Best Transport
Old City (including Sultanahmet)	Havataş airport bus, funicular & tram
Beyoğlu	Havataş airport bus
Bosphorus suburbs	Taxi

✈ At the Airports

At both international airports there are car-rental desks, exchange offices, stands of mobile-phone companies, ATMs, a tourist information desk, a left-luggage facility and a PTT (post office) in the international arrivals area.

Atatürk International Airport also has a 24-hour pharmacy.

❸ Getting Around

İstanbul has an extensive and efficient public transport system. You will save time, money and hassle by purchasing a rechargeable İstanbulkart (p147) transport card.

🚋 Tram

Services run from Bağcılar, in the city's west, to Kabataş, in Beyoğlu, stopping at the Grand Bazaar, Sultanahmet, Eminönü and Karaköy en route. Connect with the metro at Zeytinburnu and Sirkeci, with ferries at Eminönü and funiculars at Karaköy and Kabataş.

⛴ Ferry

Travel between the European and Asian shores, along the Bosphorus and Golden Horn, and to the Adalar (Princes' Islands).

Ⓜ Metro

The M1A connects Yenikapı with Atatürk International Airport; the M2 connects Yenikapı with Hacıosman via Taksim; and the Marmaray connects Kazlıçeşme, west of the Old City, with Sirkeci before crossing under the Bosphorus to Üsküdar and Ayrılık Çeşmesi.

🚕 Taxi

Inexpensive and plentiful; hail on the street.

🚡 Funicular

These make the trip from the tramline up to İstiklal Caddesi in Beyoğlu easy. One connects Karaköy with Tünel Meydanı; the other connects Kabataş with Taksim Meydanı.

🚌 Bus

Used when travelling along both sides of the Bosphorus and from Eminönü to the Western Districts.

İstanbul Neighbourhoods

Worth a Trip

👁 **Top Sights**

Kariye Museum
(Chora Church; p80)

The Bosphorus (p114)

İstiklal Caddesi & Beyoğlu (p82)

Dominated by İstiklal, the city's most famous boulevard, this high-octane neighbourhood hosts the best eating, drinking and entertainment options.

👁 **Top Sights**

İstiklal Caddesi

Pera Museum

Kariye Museum (Chora Church) 👁

İstiklal Caddesi 👁

Pera Museum 👁

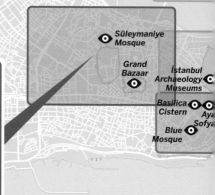

Süleymaniye Mosque 👁

Grand Bazaar 👁

İstanbul Archaeology Museums 👁

Basilica Cistern 👁 👁 Aya Sofya

Blue Mosque 👁

Grand Bazaar & the Bazaar District (p58)

A walk through this beguiling district features historic bazaars, chaotic local shopping streets and stunning imperial mosques.

👁 **Top Sights**

Grand Bazaar

Süleymaniye Mosque

Dolmabahçe Palace

The Bosphorus

Topkapı Palace & Eminönü (p42)
A profusion of parks, pavilions, museums and scenic viewpoints gives this former stomping ground of the Ottoman sultans its unique allure.

Top Sights

Topkapı Palace

İstanbul Archaeology Museums

Dolmabahçe Palace & Ortaköy (p104)
Opulent Ottoman palaces and ultrafashionable nightclubs can be found along this privileged and picturesque stretch of the Bosphorus shore.

Top Sight

Dolmabahçe Palace

Topkapı Palace

Aya Sofya & Sultanahmet (p22)
The famous Byzantine basilica is only one of many extraordinary museums and monuments in this ancient area.

Top Sights

Aya Sofya

Blue Mosque

Basilica Cistern

Explore
İstanbul

Worth a Trip

Beyoğlu street behind the Fish Market (p85), lined with
meyhanes (taverns)
AYHAN ALTUN/GETTY IMAGES ©

Explore

Aya Sofya & Sultanahmet

Many visitors to İstanbul never make it out of Sultanahmet. And while this is a shame, it's hardly surprising. After all, its mosques and museums – including the magnificent Aya Sofya, pictured – provide a time capsule of Byzantine and Ottoman history and culture unmatched anywhere in the world, and its impressive array of sights, shops and hotels are all within easy walking distance.

The Sights in a Day

☼ In İstanbul, all roads lead to the city's spiritual centre, Sultanahmet Park. Bookended by the grand edifices of Aya Sofya and the Blue Mosque, this relatively unassuming garden is built over the ruins of the Great Palace of Byzantium and is a good place to start your exploration of the neighbourhood. After visiting the **Blue Mosque** (p28), pop into the **Museum of Great Palace Mosaics** (p34), browse the shops in the **Arasta Bazaar** (p39), then make your way to **Aya Sofya** (p24 and the **Aya Sofya Tombs** (p34).

☼ After lunch at **Cooking Alaturka** (p35) or **Erol Lokantası** (p37), wander through the **Hippodrome** (p33) and into the **Museum of Turkish & Islamic Arts** (p33). Afterwards, head to the **Basilica Cistern** (p30) and then enjoy panoramic views and a pre-dinner drink at the **A'YA Rooftop Lounge** (p39) or **Cihannüma** (p39).

☾ Sample some of the city's famous fish at **Balıkçı Sabahattin** (p35) or dine on dishes fit for a sultan at **Deraliye** (p35), and then wind down with a nargile (water pipe) at **Derviş Aile Çay Bahçesi** (p38) or **Cafe Meşale** (p39).

◉ Top Sights

Aya Sofya (p24)

Blue Mosque (p28)

Basilica Cistern (p30)

♥ Best of İstanbul

Museums

Museum of Turkish & Islamic Arts (p33)

Museum of Great Palace Mosaics (p34)

Architecture

Aya Sofya (p24)

Blue Mosque (p28)

Basilica Cistern (p30)

Little Aya Sofya (p34)

Shopping

Jennifer's Hamam (p39)

Khaftan (p40)

Mehmet Çetinkaya Gallery (p40)

İznik Classics (p40)

Getting There

🚋 **Tram** Alight at the Sultanahmet stop, which is very close to Sultanahmet Park.

Top Sights
Aya Sofya

There are many important monuments in İstanbul, but this venerable structure – commissioned by the great Byzantine emperor Justinian, consecrated as a church in 537, converted to a mosque by Mehmet the Conqueror in 1453 and declared a museum by Atatürk in 1935 – surpasses the rest due to its rich history, religious importance and extraordinary beauty. Known as Hagia Sofia in Greek, Sancta Sophia in Latin and the Church of the Divine Wisdom in English, it is one of the world's greatest buildings.

👁 Map p32, D1

www.ayasofyamuzesi.gov.tr/en

Aya Sofya Meydanı 1

adult/child under 12yr ₺40/free

🕘9am-7pm Tue-Sun mid-Apr–mid-Oct, to 5pm mid-Oct–mid-Apr

🚋Sultanahmet

Dome viewed from inside

Imperial Door

The main entrance into the nave is crowned with a mosaic of Christ as Pantocrator (Ruler of All). Christ holds a book that carries the inscription 'Peace be with you. I am the Light of the World' and is flanked by the Virgin Mary and the Archangel Gabriel. At his feet an emperor (probably Leo VI) prostrates himself.

Nave

Made 'transparent' by its lack of obtrusive supporting columns, Aya Sofya's nave is as visually arresting as it is enormous. The chandeliers hanging low above the floor are Ottoman additions, as are the elevated kiosk where the sultan worshipped and the 19th-century medallions inscribed with gilt Arabic letters.

Apse

The 9th-century mosaic of the Virgin and Christ Child in the apse is the focal point of the nave. A *mimber* (pulpit) and *mihrab* (prayer niche indicating the direction of Mecca) were added by the Ottomans.

Dome

The famous dome measures 30m in diameter and 56m in height. It is supported by 40 massive ribs resting on four huge pillars concealed in the interior walls. On its completion, the Byzantine historian Procopius described it as being 'hung from heaven on a golden chain'.

Seraphs

The four huge winged angels at the base of the dome were originally mosaic, but two (on the western side) were re-created as frescoes after being damaged in the 13th century. All four faces were covered by metallic discs during the Ottoman period, and are slowly being restored.

☑ Top Tips

▶ Go during lunchtime or late in the day to beat the crowds.

▶ Buy the Museum Pass İstanbul (p152) or hire a private guide to jump the queue for admission.

▶ After exiting, head around the corner to visit the Aya Sofya Tombs (p34) and Carpet Museum (p33), both originally part of the Aya Sofya complex.

▶ Last entry is one hour before closing.

✕ Take a Break

Leafy Derviş Aile Çay Bahçesi (p38) opposite the Blue Mosque is a good spot for tea, fresh juice and people-watching.

Sip a çay at Caferağa Medresesi Çay Bahçesi (p56), a tea garden set in the courtyard of a 16th-century *medrese* (seminary) nestled in Aya Sofya's shadow.

Saints Mosaics

When in the nave, look up towards the northeast (to your left if you are facing the apse), and you will see three mosaics at the base of the northern tympanum (semicircle) beneath the dome. These are 9th-century portraits of St Ignatius the Younger, St John Chrysostom and St Ignatius Theodorus of Antioch. Next to them (but only visible from the upstairs north gallery) is a mosaic portrait of Emperor Alexandros.

Weeping Column

Legend has it that this column in the northeast aisle was blessed by St Gregory the Miracle Worker and that putting one's finger into its hole can lead to the healing of ailments, if the finger emerges moist.

Upstairs Galleries

To access the galleries, walk up the switchback ramp at the northern end of the inner narthex. When you reach the top you'll find a large circle of green marble marking the spot where the throne of the empress once stood. The view over the main space towards the apse from this vantage point is quite spectacular.

Deesis (Last Judgment)

The remnants of this magnificent 13th-century mosaic are in the up-

Aya Sofya – Ground Floor & Upstairs Galleries

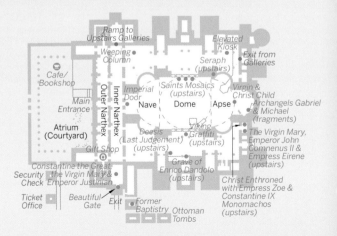

stairs south gallery. It depicts Christ with the Virgin Mary on his left and John the Baptist on his right.

Grave of Enrico Dandolo

Dandolo, who was Doge of Venice, led the soldiers of the Fourth Crusade who conquered Constantinople in 1204. He died in the city the following year, and was buried in Aya Sofya's upper gallery. A 19th-century marker indicates the probable location of his grave.

Christ Enthroned with Empress Zoe & Constantine IX Monomachos

This mosaic portrait in the upper gallery depicts Zoe (r 1042), one of only three Byzantine women to rule as empress in their own right.

The Virgin Mary, Emperor John Comnenus II & Empress Eirene

A wonderful mosaic featuring 'John the Good' on the Virgin's left and his wife Eirene, who was known for her charitable works, on the Virgin's right. Their son Alexius, who died soon after the portrait was made, is depicted next to Eirene.

Viking Graffiti

Graffiti dating from the 9th century is carved into a marble banister in the upstairs south balcony. It is thought to have been the work of a mercenary called Halvdan.

Virgin & Christ Child mosaic

Constantine the Great, the Virgin Mary & Emperor Justinian

As you exit the building, don't miss this 10th-century mosaic showing Constantine (right) offering the Virgin Mary the city of Constantinople; Justinian (left) is offering her Hagia Sophia.

Ottoman Tombs

The beautifully decorated tombs (p33) of five Ottoman sultans and their families are located in Aya Sofya's southern corner and accessed via Kabasakal Caddesi. One of the tombs occupies the original church's Baptistry.

Top Sights
Blue Mosque

İstanbul's most photogenic building was the grand project of Sultan Ahmet I (r 1603–17), whose *türbe* (tomb) is located on the northern side of the site facing Sultanahmet Park and Aya Sofya. The mosque's wonderfully curvaceous exterior features a huge courtyard, a cascade of domes and six slender minarets (more than any other Ottoman mosque). Inside, thousands of blue İznik tiles adorn the walls and give the building its unofficial but commonly used name.

Sultanahmet Camii

👁 Map p32, C3

📞 0545 577 1899

www.bluemosque.co

Hippodrome

🕑 closed to non-worshippers during six daily prayer times

🚊 Sultanahmet

Prayer hall

The Ceremonial Entrance

The mosque is best approached via the Hippo-drome. When entering the courtyard, you'll be able to appreciate the perfect proportions of the building and see how a progression of domes draws worshippers' eyes from ground level (ie earth) to the dome and minarets (ie heaven).

Prayer Hall

The 260 stained-glass windows and mass of İznik tiles immediately attract attention, and the dome and semidomes are painted with graceful arabesques. Notable structures include an elevated kiosk covered with marble latticework; a *mihrab* featuring a piece of the sacred Black Stone from the Kaaba in Mecca; a high *mahfil* (chair) from which the imam gives the sermon on Fridays; and a beautifully carved white-marble *mimber*.

The Mosque Complex

Imperial mosques usually incorporated public service institutions such as hospitals, soup kitchens and hamams. Here, a large *medrese* (Islamic school of higher studies; closed to the public) and *arasta* (row of shops by a mosque; now the Arasta Bazaar) remain. The rent from shops in the *arasta* has traditionally supported the upkeep of the mosque; the best shopping in Sultanahmet is found in and around this historic arcade.

Tomb of Sultan Ahmet I

Ahmet died one year after his mosque was constructed, aged only 27. Buried with him are his wife, Kösem, who was strangled to death in the Topkapı Harem, and his sons, Sultan Osman II, Sultan Murat IV and Prince Beyazıt (strangled by order of Murat). Like the mosque, the tomb features fine İznik tiles.

☑ **Top Tips**

▶ The mosque is closed to non-worshippers during the six daily prayer times.

▶ Only worshippers are admitted through the main eastern door; tourists must use the southern door (follow the signs).

▶ Women who don't have a headscarf or are considered to be too scantily dressed will be lent a headscarf and/or chador.

▶ Shoes must be removed before entering the prayer hall; it's best to carry them with you in a plastic bag (provided) rather than leaving them on the shelves.

✗ **Take a Break**

Enjoy a çay at Cafe Meşale (p39) in the Arasta Bazaar.

Sample some classic Turkish dishes over lunch at Cooking Alaturka (p35).

Top Sights
Basilica Cistern

Commissioned by Emperor Justinian, this subterranean structure was built in 532 beneath the Stoa Basilica, a great square that occupied Byzantium's First Hill. The largest surviving Byzantine cistern in İstanbul, it features a forest of 336 marble and granite columns, many of which were salvaged from ruined classical temples and have fine carved capitals. The cistern's symmetry and sheer grandeur of conception are quite breathtaking, making it a favourite location for big-budget films (remember *From Russia With Love*?).

Yerebatan Sarnıçı

👁 Map p32, C1

www.yerebatan.com

Yerebatan Caddesi

admission ₺20

🕙 9am-6.30pm mid-Apr–Sep, to 5.30pm Nov–mid-Apr

🚊 Sultanahmet

Base of Medusa-head column

Columns

The cistern's columns are all 9m high; most have Ionic or Corinthian capitals. Arranged in 12 rows, they include one column which has been engraved with shapes that are often described as peacock's eyes, or tears. Some historians assert that these tears were carved to pay tribute to the hundreds of slaves who died during the construction of the cistern.

Medusa Heads

Two columns feature striking bases carved with the head of Medusa. One is upside down, the other on its side. When the building functioned as a cistern, both would have lain beneath the surface of the water. Now revealed, they provide the building with an element of mystery.

The Fish

The cistern was built to store water for the Great Palace of Byzantium, a sprawling complex occupying the area between the Hippodrome and the Sea of Marmara. After the Turkish conquest of İstanbul (the Conquest), it supplied water to irrigate the gardens of Topkapı Palace. Decommissioned in the 19th century, its shallow water is now home to ghostly patrols of carp and goldfish that can be seen from the cistern's elevated wooden walkways.

☑ Top Tips

▶ The cistern is a blissfully cool retreat on hot summer days – visit in the afternoon, when the city's heat can be particularly oppressive.

▶ Watch young children carefully, as the walkways over the water don't have much of a safety barrier.

✕ Take a Break

Çiğdem Pastanesi (p37) is a good spot to enjoy a coffee or tea accompanied by a *börek*, cake or milk-based pudding.

For a cheap and tasty lunch, head to nearby Erol Lokantası (p37), a popular *lokanta* (eatery serving ready-made food) – try to arrive at the start of service, as dishes can sell out quickly.

For reviews see
Top Sights   p24
Sights   p33
Eating   p35
Drinking   p38
Shopping   p39

200 m
0.1 miles

Sea of Marmara

Kennedy Cad (Sahil Yolu)

Ahırkapı Sk

Yenigün Sk

Şadırvan Çık

İshakpaşa Cad

CANKURTARAN

Adliye Sk

Terbıyık Sk

Kutluğun Sk

Akbıyık Cad

Bayram Firini Sk

Cankurtaran Cad

Amiral Tafdil Sk

Kılıçarslan Maha

Kereatsci Başkı Sk

Aya Sofya
Tombs

Soğukçeşme
Sk

Aya Sofya

Babıhümayun Cad

Aya Sofya
Meydanı

Caferiye Sk

Kabasakal Cad

Tevkifhane Sk

Utangaç Sk

SULTANAHMET

Mimar Mehmet Ağa Cad

Ağa Çk

Arasta Bazaar

Torun Sk

Minas Sk

Akbıyık Değirmen Sk

Tomurcuk Sk

Museum of
Great Palace
Mosaics

Küçük Ayasofya Cad

Basilica
Cistern

Alemdar Cad

Sultanahmet
Park

Dalbastı Sk

Tomb of
Sultan Ahmet I

Blue
Mosque

Şifa
Hamamı
Sk

Tavukhane Sk

Nakilbent Sk

Kapıağası Sk

Yeşil Sk

Yerebatan Cad

Seftali Sk

ALEMDAR

Ticarethane Sk

Sultanahmet

BİNBİRDİREK

İmran Öktem Cad

Atmeydanı Cad

Hippodrome

Museum of
Turkish &
Islamic Arts

Üçler Sk

Nakkaş

Terzihane Sk

Küçük Ayasofya
Camii Sk

Kaleci Sk

KÜÇÜK
AYASOFYA

Little Aya

Sakal Cad

Kasap Osman Sk

Nakilbent Sk

Su Terazisi Sk

Dizdariye Çeşmesi Sk

Peykhane Cad

Klodfarer Cad

Işık Sk

Dr Şevkibey
Sk

Bab-ı Ali Cad

Divan Yolu Cad

Çatal Çeşme Sk

Türbedar Sk

Boyacı Ahmet Sk

Piyer Loti Cad

Göktaş Sk

Katip Sinan Camii Sk

Dizdariye Çeşmesi Sk

Obelisk of Theodosius, Hippodrome

Sights

Museum of Turkish & Islamic Arts

MUSEUM

1 ◉ Map p32, B2

This Ottoman palace was built in 1524 for İbrahim Paşa, childhood friend, brother-in-law and grand vizier of Süleyman the Magnificent. Recently renovated, it has a magnificent collection of artefacts, including exquisite calligraphy and one of the world's most impressive antique carpet collections. Some large-scale carpets have been moved to the **Carpet Museum** (Halı Müzesi; ☑0212-518 1330; www.halimuzesi.com; cnr Babıhümayun Caddesi & Soğukçeşme Sokak; admission ₺10; ☉9am-6pm Tue-Sun

mid-Apr–mid-Oct, to 4pm mid-Oct–mid-Apr) from the upper rooms, but the collection remains a knockout with its palace carpets, prayer rugs and glittering artefacts such as a 17th-century Ottoman incense burner. (Türk ve İslam Eserleri Müzesi; www.tiem.gov.tr; Atmeydanı Caddesi 46, Hippodrome; adult/child under 12yr ₺25/free; ☉9am-5pm Nov–mid-Apr, to 7pm mid-Apr–Oct, last entry 30mins before closing; 🚇Sultanahmet)

Hippodrome

PARK

2 ◉ Map p32, B2

The Byzantine Emperors loved nothing more than an afternoon at the chariot races, and this rectangular arena alongside Sultanahmet Park was their venue of choice. In its heyday, it was decorated by obelisks and statues, some of which remain in place today. Re-landscaped in more recent years, it is one of the city's most popular meeting places and promenades. (Atmeydanı; Atmeydanı Caddesi; 🚇Sultanahmet)

Aya Sofya Tombs   TOMB

3 ◉ Map p32, D2

Part of the Aya Sofya complex but entered via Babıhümayun Caddesi, these tombs are the final resting places of five 16th- and 17th-century sultans – Mehmet III, Selim II, Murat III, İbrahim I and Mustafa I – most of whom are buried with members of their families. The ornate interior decoration in the tombs features the very best Ottoman tile work, calligraphy and decorative paintwork. (Aya Sofya Müzesi Padişah Türbeleri; 🕿0212-522 1750; http://ayasofyamuzesi.gov.tr/en; Babıhümayun Caddesi; admission free; ⊙9am-5pm; 🚇Sultanahmet)

Tomb of Sultan Ahmet I   TOMB

4 ◉ Map p32, C2

The *türbe* (tomb) of Sultan Ahmet I, the Blue Mosque's great patron, is on the north side of the mosque facing Sultanahmet Park. Ahmet, who had ascended to the imperial throne aged 13, died at just 27 years, one year after the mosque was constructed. Like the mosque, the *türbe* features fine İznik tiles. (Kabasakal Caddesi; admission free; ⊙9.30am-4.30pm; 🚇Sultanahmet)

Museum of Great Palace Mosaics   MUSEUM

5 ◉ Map p32, C4

When archaeologists from the University of Ankara and Scotland's University of St Andrews excavated around nearby Arasta Bazaar in the 1930s and 1950s, they uncovered a stunning mosaic pavement featuring mythological and hunting scenes. Dating from early Byzantine times, it was restored over 15 years and is now preserved in this museum. (🕿0212-518 1205; www.ayasofyamuzesi.gov.tr/en/museum-great-palace-mosaics; Torun Sokak; admission ₺15; ⊙9am-7pm mid-Apr–Sep, to 5pm Oct–mid-Apr, last entry 30min before closing; 🚇Sultanahmet)

Little Aya Sofya   MOSQUE

6 ◉ Map p32, A4

Justinian and his wife Theodora built this little church sometime between 527 and 536, just before Justinian built Aya Sofya. You can still see their monogram worked into some of the frilly white capitals. The building is one of the most beautiful Byzantine structures in the city despite being converted into a mosque in the early 16th century and having many of its original features obscured during an extensive restoration in 2007. (Küçük Aya Sofya Camii, SS Sergius & Bacchus Church; Küçük Ayasofya Caddesi; admission free; ⊙sunrise-sunset; 🚇Sultanahmet or Çemberlitaş)

Nakkaş
MUSEUM

7 👁 Map p32, B4

This renovated 6th-century cistern houses exhibits of virtual and physical models that recreate the nearby Hippodrome as it was in its heyday. Also interesting is the bird's-eye view of Constantinople in 1200, when the Great Palace of Byzantium and the Hippodrome dominated present-day Sultanahmet. When we visited, there were plans to make this informative exhibition permanent. (☏0212-516 5222; www.nakkasrug.com; Nakilbent Sokak 13; admission free; ⊙9am-7pm; 🚋Sultanahmet)

Eating

Balıkçı Sabahattin
SEAFOOD €€€

8 🍴 Map p32, D3

Balıkçı Sabahattin is an enduring favourite with discerning Turks from near and far, who enjoy the limited menu of meze and seafood, including fish from red mullet to sole. This is Sultanahmet's most prestigious restaurant and its best food, although the service can be harried. You'll dine under a leafy canopy in the garden (one section smoking, the other non-smoking). (☏0212-458 1824; www.balikcisabahattin.com; Şeyit Hasan Koyu Sokak 1, Cankurtaran; mezes ₺10-40, fish ₺40-60; ⊙11am-10pm; 🛜; 🚋Sultanahmet)

Deraliye
OTTOMAN €€€

9 🍴 Map p32, B1

Starting with a complimentary glass of palate-titillating pomegranate-flower juice, Deraliye offers a taste of the sumptuous dishes once served in the great Ottoman palaces. The menu gives a potted history of each dish, so you can live out your royal banquet fantasies by ordering the goose kebap served to Süleyman the Magnificent or Mehmet II's favourite lamb stew. (☏0212-520 7778; www.deraliyerestaurant.com; Ticarethane Sokak 10; mains ₺34-64; ⊙11am-10pm; 🛜🍴; 🚋Sultanahmet)

Ahırkapı Balıkçısı
SEAFOOD €€€

10 🍴 Map p32, D4

Join the locals at this tiny and authentically Turkish neighbourhood fish restaurant where a seafood-packed fridge beckons to a quiet cobbled street. Get here early to score a table, especially at dinner. (☏0212-518 4988; Keresteci Hakkı Sokak 46, Cankurtaran; mezes ₺5-40, fish ₺35-80; ⊙noon-11pm; 🛜; 🚋Sultanahmet)

Cooking Alaturka
TURKISH €€€

11 🍴 Map p32, D3

One of the Sultanahmet area's best dining experiences, this hybrid cooking-school–restaurant serves a set four- or five-course menu of Turkish home-cooking, regional Anatolian specialities and Ottoman classics. Sampling dishes such as *imam bayıldı* ('the imam fainted'; eggplant, onion, tomato and peppers slow-cooked in olive oil) with

Understand

Byzantium

Known for its charismatic emperors, powerful armies, refined culture and convoluted politics, Byzantium's legacy resonates to this day.

The Eastern Roman Empire

Legend tells us that the city of Byzantium was founded in 667 BC by a group of colonists from Megara, northwest of Athens, led by Byzas, the son of Megara's king. An alliance was eventually formed with the Romans, and the city was officially incorporated into their empire in AD 79. In the late 3rd century, Emperor Diocletian (r 284–305) split the empire into eastern and western administrative units. His actions resulted in a civil war in which a rival, Constantine I, triumphed. Constantine made Byzantium his capital in 330, naming it 'New Rome'.

The new capital soon came to be known as Constantinople. Constantine died in 337, but the city continued to grow under the rule of emperors including Theodosius I ('the Great'; r 379–95), Theodosius II (r 408–50) and Justinian (r 527–65). The eastern and western empires had been politically separated after the death of Theodosius I, but the final tie with Rome wasn't severed until 620, when Heraclius I (r 610–41) changed the official language of the eastern empire from Latin to Greek, inaugurating what we now refer to as the 'Byzantine Empire'.

The Byzantine Empire

For the next eight centuries the empire asserted its independence from Rome by adopting Orthodox Christianity. Ruled by a series of family dynasties, it was the most powerful economic, cultural and military force in Europe until the Seljuk Turks acquired much of its territory in Asia Minor in 1071.

In 1204 Constantinople fell to Latin soldiers of the Fourth Crusade. The powerful Byzantine families went into exile in Nicaea and Epirus, and the empire was split between Greek and Latin factions. Despite being reclaimed by the Nicaean emperor Michael VIII Palaiologos in 1261, it was plagued by a series of civil wars and finally fell to the Ottomans in 1453, when Mehmet II (Fatih, or Conqueror) took Constantinople. The last Byzantine emperor, Constantine XI Palaiologos, died defending the walls from Mehmet's onslaught.

Pide (Turkish-style pizza)

a glass of local wine is a wonderful way to experience authentic Turkish cuisine. (☎0212-458 5919; www.cookingalaturka.com; Akbıyık Caddesi 72a, Cankurtaran; set lunch or dinner ₺65; ⊙lunch 1-3pm & dinner 7-9pm by reservation Mon-Sat; 🛜✏; 🚇Sultanahmet)

Erol Lokantası
TURKISH €

12 🍴 Map p32, B1

One of Sultanahmet's last *lokantas* (eateries serving ready-made food), Erol wouldn't win any awards for its interior design but might for its warm welcome and food. The dishes in the bain-marie are made fresh daily using seasonal ingredients by the Erol family members, who have collectively put in several decades in the kitchen. (☎0212-511 0322; Çatal Çeşme Sokak 3, Cağaloğlu; portions ₺5.50-15.50; ⊙11am-9pm Mon-Sat; ✏; 🚇Sultanahmet)

Çiğdem Pastanesi
CAFE €

13 🍴 Map p32, B1

Strategically located on the main drag between Aya Sofya Meydanı and the Grand Bazaar, Çiğdem has been tempting locals since 1961 with its mouthwatering window display of gateaux and pastries. Pop in for a quick tea (₺2.50) or coffee (flat white ₺7.50) accompanied by *börek* (filled pastries), baklava or *tavuk göğsü* (a dessert made from milk, rice and pounded chicken breast). (Divan Yolu Caddesi 62a; pastries ₺1.50-7.50, cakes ₺3-10; ⊙7.30am-11.30pm; 🚇Sultanahmet)

WIBOWO RUSLI/GETTY IMAGES ©

Karadeniz Aile Pide ve Kebap Salonu
PIDE, KEBAP €

14 🍴 Map p32, B1

Serving tasty pides and kebaps since 1985, the original Karadeniz (Black Sea)–style pide joint in this enclave is a hit with local shopkeepers. You can claim a table in the utilitarian interior (women usually sit upstairs) or on the lane. No alcohol. (☎0212-522 9191; www.karadenizpide.net; Hacı Tahsinbey Sokak 7, off Divan Yolu Caddesi; pides ₺16-24, kebaps ₺18-32; ⏱11am-10pm; 🚆Sultanahmet)

Palatium
PIDE, TURKISH €€

15 🍴 Map p32, D3

Palatium is built atop part of the Great Palace of Byzantium, which you can see through its glass floor, between the rugs, beanbag seats at low tables and dangling lanterns. While the food is better than at many of the surrounding tourist haunts, the pide is probably the best choice, making Palatium better for lunch or a snack than dinner. (☎0543 844 5413; www.palatiumcafeandrestaurant.com; Kutlugün Sokak 33; mezes ₺11, pides ₺23, mains ₺30; ⏱11am-10pm; 🛜🚭; 🚆Sultanahmet)

Tarihi Sultanahmet Köftecisi Selim Usta
KÖFTE €

16 🍴 Map p32, C1

Not to be confused with the nearby Meşhur Sultanahmet Köftecisi, this no-frills place near the Sultanahmet tram stop is the most famous eatery in the Old City. It has been serving its slightly rubbery *ızgara köfte* (grilled meatballs) and bean salad to ultra-loyal locals since 1920, and shows no sign of losing its custom – there's often a queue outside. (☎0212-520 0566; www.sultanahmetkoftesi.com; Divan Yolu Caddesi 12; köfte ₺16, beans ₺7, çorba ₺5; ⏱11am-10pm; 🚆Sultanahmet)

Drinking

Derviş Aile Çay Bahçesi
TEA GARDEN

17 ☕ Map p32, C2

Superbly located directly opposite the Blue Mosque, the Derviş beckons patrons with its comfortable cane chairs and shady trees. Efficient service, reasonable prices and peerless people-watching opportunities make it a great place for a leisurely çay (₺3), nargile (₺22), *tost* (toasted sandwich; ₺7) and a game of backgammon. (cnr Dalbastı Sokak

& Kabasakal Caddesi; ⊙7am-midnight Apr-Oct; 🚇Sultanahmet)

Cafe Meşale
NARGILE CAFE

18 🚇 Map p32, C3

Located in a sunken courtyard behind the Blue Mosque, Meşale is a tourist trap *par excellence,* but still has loads of charm. Generations of backpackers have joined locals in claiming one of its cushioned benches and enjoying a tea and nargile. It has sporadic live Turkish music and a bustling vibe in the evening. (Arasta Bazaar, cnr Dalbastı & Torun Sokaks, Cankurtaran; ⊙24hr; 🚇Sultanahmet)

A'YA Rooftop Lounge
BAR

19 🚇 Map p32, D2

Open in summer, this rooftop bar has a full-on view of Aya Sofya, Ayasofya Hürrem Sultan Hamamı and the Bosphorus, while the Blue Mosque is only partially obscured. Cocktails (₺49), meze (₺30) and an impressive selection of spirits add to the appeal. In winter, sit downstairs in the lounge bar or courtyard garden. (📞0212-402 3000; www.fourseasons.com/istanbul; Four Seasons Istanbul at Sultanahmet, Tevkifhane Sokak 1, Cankurtaran; ⊙4pm-late; 🚇Sultanahmet)

Cihannüma
BAR

20 🚇 Map p32, C1

We don't recommend eating at this rooftop hotel restaurant near Aya Sofya, but the view from its narrow balcony and glass-sheathed dining room is one of the Old City's best (spot Aya Sofya,

Blue Mosque, Topkapı Palace, Galata Tower and the Bosphorus Bridge), so it's a great choice for a scenic afternoon drink or sundowner. (📞0212-512 0207; www.cihannumaistanbul.com; And Hotel, Yerebatan Caddesi 18; ⊙noon-midnight; 🚇Sultanahmet)

Kybele Cafe
BAR, CAFE

21 🚇 Map p32, C1

The hotel lounge bar–cafe close to the Basilica Cistern is chock-full of antique furniture, richly coloured rugs and old etchings and prints, but its signature style comes courtesy of the hundreds of colourful glass lights hanging from the ceiling. (📞0212-511 7766; www.kybele hotel.com; Yerebatan Caddesi 23; ⊙7.30am-11.30pm; 🚇Sultanahmet)

Shopping

Jennifer's Hamam
BATHWARES, HOMEWARES

22 🔒 Map p32, B4

Owned by Canadian Jennifer Gaudet, this shop stocks top-quality hamam items, including towels, robes and *peştemals* (bath wraps) produced using certified organic cotton and silk on old-style shuttled looms. It also sells natural soaps and *keses* (coarse cloth mittens used for exfoliation). Prices are set; no bargaining. This is the main showroom; there are two further **branches** at numbers 125 and 135 in the Arasta Bazaar. (📞0212-516 3022; www.jennifershamam.com; Öğül Sokak

20; ⊗8.30am-9pm Apr-Oct, to 7pm Nov-Mar; 🚇Sultanahmet)

Khaftan   ART, ANTIQUES

23 🔒 Map p32, B4

Gleaming Russian icons, delicate calligraphy (old and new), ceramics, *karagöz* (shadow-puppet theatre) puppets, Ottoman prints and contemporary paintings are all on show in this attractive shop. (📞0212-458 5425; Nakilbent Sokak 16; ⊗9am-7pm; 🚇Sultanahmet)

Mehmet Çetinkaya Gallery   CARPETS, JEWELLERY

24 🔒 Map p32, C4

Mehmet Çetinkaya is one of the country's foremost experts on antique

🔍 Local Life
Küçük Ayasofya

The streets around Aya Sofya and the Blue Mosque are predominantly populated with hotels, restaurants and shops catering to tourists. To dodge the touts and tour groups that congregate here, head to the southern end of the Hippodrome and walk down Şehit Mehmet Paşa Yokuşu and Katip Sinan Camii Sokak to reach Kadırga Limanı Caddesi in the vibrant residential neighbourhood of Küçük Ayasofya. Turn right to reach Kadırga Park, a popular local meeting place with benches under leafy trees and plenty of playground equipment for children. A number of inexpensive teahouses and cafes are nearby.

oriental carpets and kilims. Built over a Byzantine well, his flagship store-cum-gallery stocks items of artistic and ethnographic significance, and is full of treasures including carpets, kilims, textiles and jewellery. A **branch** at Arasta Bazaar 58 sells textiles and antique jewellery. (📞0212-517 1603, 0212-517 6808; www.cetinkayagallery.com; Tavukhane Sokak 5-7; ⊗9am-8pm; 🚇Sultanahmet)

İznik Classics   CERAMICS

25 🔒 Map p32, D3

İznik Classics is one of the best places in town to source hand-painted collector-item ceramics made with real quartz and using metal oxides for pigments. Admire the range here or at **branches** at number 119 Arasta Bazaar (📞0212-517 3608; 🚇Sultanahment) and the Grand Bazaar (📞0212-520 2568; Şerifağa Sokak 188, İç Bedesten; ⊗8.30am-7pm Mon-Sat; 🚇Beyazıt-Kapalı Çarşı). The shop next door at number 13 sells Kütahya ceramics, including tiles, plates and bowls. (📞0212-516 8874; www.iznikclassics.com; Utangaç Sokak 17; ⊗9am-8pm, closes 6.30pm winter; 🚇Sultanahmet)

Cocoon   CARPETS, TEXTILES

26 🔒 Map p32, C4

Sultanahmet is thickly carpeted with rug and textile shops but Cocoon is worth a look. Felt hats, felt-and-silk scarves, rugs, cushion covers and textiles from central Asia are artfully displayed. (📞0212-518 0338; www.yastk.com; Küçük Ayasofya Caddesi 17; ⊗9am-6pm; 🚇Sultanahmet)

İznik-style ceramics

Yilmaz Ipekçilik   TEXTILES

27 🏢 Map p32, C3

The Büyükaşık family specialises in well-priced hand-loomed silk textiles made in Antakya. They have been at it for several generations, producing good-quality scarves, shawls and *peştemals* (bath wraps). (📞0212-638 4579; www.yilmazipekcilik.com/en; Torun Sokak 3; 🕙9am-9pm Mon-Sat, to 7pm winter; 🚊Sultanahmet)

Galeri Kayseri   BOOKS

28 🏢 Map p32, B1

Peddling literature since 1996, these twin shops stock a well-presented selection of English-language novels, history books, maps and coffee-table tomes on Turkey, and have knowledgeable staff on hand to recommend a good holiday read. The second, smaller, shop is on the opposite side of the road half a block closer to Aya Sofya. (📞0212-516 3366; www.galerikayseri.com; Divan Yolu Caddesi 11 & 58; 🕙9am-8pm; 🚊Sultanahmet)

Explore

Topkapı Palace & Eminönü

The leafy parks and gardens in and around opulent Ottoman-era Topkapı Palace, pictured, stand in stark contrast to the crowded shopping streets clustered around the Eminönü ferry docks, but both areas are full of life and well worth a visit. Topkapı ıs perenni-ally packed with tourists and Eminönü with locals; between them lies Gülhane Park, a tranquil retreat popular with both groups.

The Sights in a Day

Topkapı Palace (p104) is one of Turkey's most compelling cultural attractions so you'll need at least half a day to do it justice; start early to make the most of your time. After exploring all four courtyards of this historically significant landmark, make sure you detour into **Soğukçeşme Sokak** (p52) to admire one of the city's prettiest streetscapes and visit the impressive **Carpet Museum** (p51).

After joining the locals for lunch at one of the eateries on **Hocapaşa Sokak** (p56), backtrack to the **İstanbul Archaeology Museums** (p48), home to the palace collections acquired by the sultans. Afterwards, wander through flower-filled **Gülhane Park** (p52) before heading to Eminönü to stock up on *lokum* (Turkish delight) at one of the city's oldest shops, **Ali Muhiddin Hacı Bekir** (p57).

Watch dervishes whirl at the **Hodjapasha Cultural Centre** (p57) and then walk or tram over the Galata Bridge to Beyoğlu for drinks and dinner.

Top Sights

Topkapı Palace (p104)

İstanbul Archaeology Museums (p48)

Best of İstanbul

Architecture
Topkapı Palace (p104)

Museums
İstanbul Archaeology Museums (p48)

Carpet Museum (p51)

Shopping
Özlem Tuna (p57)

Ali Muhiddin Hacı Bekir (p57)

Hafız Mustafa (p56)

Getting There

🚋 **Tram** Alight at Sultanahmet for Topkapı Palace and at Gülhane for the İstanbul Archaeology Museums and Gülhane Park.

Top Sights
Topkapı Palace

Topkapı Sarayı is the subject of more colourful stories than most of the world's museums put together. Powerful and libidinous sultans, ambitious courtiers, beautiful concubines and scheming eunuchs lived and worked here between the 15th and 19th centuries when the palace was the seat of the Ottoman sultanate. Visiting its opulent pavilions, landscaped courtyards, jewel-filled Treasury and sprawling Harem gives a fascinating glimpse into the lives of the sultans and their families, as well as offering an insight into the history and customs of a once mighty empire.

👁 Map p50, D3

www.topkapisarayi.gov.tr

Babıhümayun Caddesi

palace adult/child under 12yr ₺40/free, Harem adult/child under 6yr ₺25/free

🕑9am-6.45pm Wed-Mon mid-Apr–Oct, to 4.45pm Nov–mid-Apr

🚊Sultanahmet

Baghdad Kiosk on the Marble Terrace (p46)

First Court

Before you enter the Imperial Gate (Bab-ı Hümayun), pause to view the gorgeous rococo-style Fountain of Sultan Ahmet III in the middle of the cobbled roundabout. Passing through the gate, you will enter the Court of the Janissaries, also known as the First Court. On your left is the Byzantine church of Hagia Eirene, more commonly known as Aya İrini (p51).

Second Court

The second of the palace's huge courtyards is home to audience pavilions, barracks and the huge and recently restored palace kitchens. Be sure to visit the Outer Treasury, where an impressive collection of Ottoman and European armour is displayed.

Imperial Council Chamber

This ornate chamber on the left (west) side of the Second Court is where the Imperial Divân (Council) made laws, citizens presented petitions and foreign dignitaries were presented to the court. The sultan eavesdropped on proceedings through the gold grille high in the wall.

Harem

This complex on the western side of the Second Court was the private quarters of the sultans and their families. It features many opulently decorated bed chambers, reception rooms, hamams and courtyards. Highlights include the Salon of the Valide, Imperial Hall, Privy Chamber of Murat III, Privy Chamber of Ahmet III and Twin Kiosk/Apartments of the Crown Prince.

Third Court

The Third Court is entered through the impressive Gate of Felicity, a rococo-style structure that was used for state ceremonies including the

☑ **Top Tips**

▶ You'll need two tickets – one to the palace and another for the Harem. Both can be purchased at the main ticket office just outside the gate to the Second Court.

▶ The palace can be accessed from both the Gülhane and Sultanah-met tram stops, but note that it's a steep uphill walk from Gülhane.

▶ Arrive early and go straight to the Harem to beat the crowds.

▶ Last entry is 45 minutes before closing.

✗ **Take a Break**

The simple Sefa Restaurant (p55) serves delicious and authentic Turkish *hazır yemek* (ready-made dishes) at lunch.

Head to local institution Hafız Mustafa (p56) for a mid-afternoon sugar hit.

sultan's accession and funeral. Behind it was the sultan's private domain, staffed and guarded by eunuchs.

Audience Chamber
Important officials and foreign ambassadors were brought to this pavilion for imperial audiences. The sultan, seated on cushions embroidered with hundreds of seed pearls, inspected the ambassadors' gifts and offerings as they were passed through the small doorway on the left.

Library of Ahmet III
Directly behind the Audience Chamber is this pretty library, built in 1719 for Sultan Ahmet III. Light-filled, it has comfortable reading areas and stunning inlaid woodwork.

Costume Collection
On the eastern edge of the Third Court is the Dormitory of the Expeditionary Force, which now houses a rich collection of imperial robes, kaftans and uniforms worked in silver and gold thread. Also here is a fascinating collection of talismanic shirts, which were believed to protect the wearer from enemies and misfortunes.

Sacred Safekeeping Rooms
Sumptuously decorated with İznik tiles, these rooms are a repository for many sacred relics. When the sultans lived here, the rooms were only opened once a year on the 15th day of the holy month of Ramazan.

Dormitory of the Privy Chamber
This dormitory next to the Sacred Safekeeping Rooms now houses portraits of 36 sultans. It includes a wonderful painting of the *Enthronment Ceremony of Sultan Selim III* (1789) by court painter Kostantin Kapidagi.

Imperial Treasury
The Treasury's most famous exhibit is the Topkapı Dagger, which features three enormous emeralds on its hilt. Also here is the Kaşıkçı (Spoonmaker's) Diamond, a teardrop-shaped 86-carat rock surrounded by dozens of smaller stones. First worn by Mehmet IV at his accession to the throne in 1648, it's one of the largest diamonds in the world.

Marble Terrace
This gorgeous terrace in the Fourth Court is home to the Baghdad and Revan Kiosks, wonderful examples of classical palace architecture built in 1636 and 1639 respectively. The smaller Sünnet Odası (Circumcision Room) dates from 1640 and has outer walls covered with particularly beautiful İznik tiles.

İftariye Kameriyesi
During Ramazan, the sultans would enjoy their *iftar* (breaking of the fast) under this gilded canopy overlooking the Bosphorus and Golden Horn (Haliç). These days it's a popular location for happy snaps.

Topkapı Palace

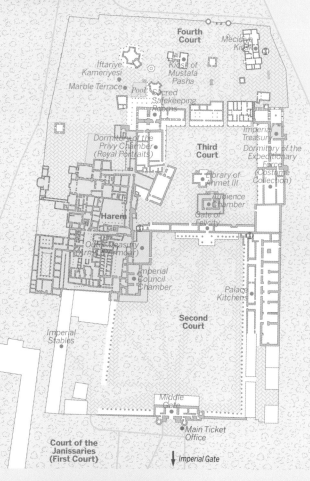

Fourth
Court

Mecidiye
Kiosk

Iftariye
Kameriyesi

Kiosk of
Mustafa
Pasha

Marble Terrace

Pool

Sacred
Safekeeping
Rooms

Dormitory of the
Privy Chamber
(Royal Portraits)

Third
Court

Imperial
Treasury

Dormitory of the
Expeditionary
Force
(Costume
Collection)

Library of
Ahmet III

Audience
Chamber

Harem

Gate of
Felicity

Outer Treasury
(Arms & Armour)

Imperial
Council
Chamber

Palace
Kitchens

Imperial
Stables

Second
Court

Middle
Gate

Main Ticket
Office

Court of the
Janissaries
(First Court)

↓ Imperial Gate

Top Sights
İstanbul Archaeology Museums

This superb museum complex houses archaeological and artistic treasures from the Imperial collections. Housed in three buildings, its exhibits include ancient artefacts, classical statuary and a fascinating exhibition tracing İstanbul's history. There are many highlights, but the sarcophagi from the Royal Necropolis of Sidon in the Archaeology Museum are particularly striking.

Archaeology Museum
This imposing neoclassical building is the heart of the museum complex. It houses an extensive

İstanbul Arkeoloji Müzeleri

👁 Map p50, C3

www.istanbularkeoloji.gov.tr

Osman Hamdi Bey Yokuşu Sokak, Gülhane

adult/child under 12yr ₺20/free

🕑 9am-7pm, last entry 6pm

🚋 Gülhane

Entrance to the Archaeology Museum

collection of classical statuary and sarcophagi, including the extraordinary Alexander Sarcophagus from the Royal Necropolis of Sidon, carved out of Pentelic marble and dating from the last quarter of the 4th century BC.

The Columned Sarcophagi of Anatolia
Amazingly detailed sarcophagi dating from between AD 140 and 270 feature in this exhibit. Many look like tiny temples or residential buildings; don't miss the Sidamara Sarcophagus from Konya.

İstanbul Through the Ages
Tracing the city's history using objects and interpretive panels, this fascinating albeit dusty exhibition on the upstairs level of the Archaeology Museum traces the city's history through its neighbourhoods during different periods: Archaic, Hellenistic, Roman, Byzantine and Ottoman.

Museum of the Ancient Orient
To your immediate left as you enter the complex, this 1883 building showcases a collection of pre-Islamic items collected from the expanse of the Ottoman Empire. Highlights include a series of large blue-and-yellow glazed-brick panels that once lined the processional street and the Ishtar Gate of ancient Babylon.

Tiled Pavilion
Built in 1472 as part of the Topkapı complex, this pavilion was originally used for watching sporting events but now houses an impressive collection of Seljuk, Anatolian and Ottoman tiles.

☑ Top Tips

▶ The complex can be easily reached by walking down the slope from Topkapı's First Court, or by walking up the hill from the main gate of Gülhane Park.

▶ If possible, visit the museum and Topkapı Palace on separate days – jamming them into a one-day itinerary may result in museum meltdown.

▶ The Archaeology Museum is the largest section, requiring the most time, followed by the Museum of the Ancient Orient.

▶ Last entry is one hour before closing.

✕ Take a Break

Stroll through Gülhane Park to Gülhane Kandil Tesisleri (p55), where you can enjoy a coffee or çay on its garden terrace.

The cheap and tasty eateries on or around Hocapaşa Sokak (p56) in Sirkeci are perfect lunch venues.

Sarayburnu

Kennedy Cad (Sahil Yolu)

İstanbul Museum of
the History of Science &
Technology in Islam

Topkapı
Palace

Gülhane
Park

İstanbul
Archaeology
Museums

Ahmet Hamdi
Tanpınar Literature
Museum Library

Aya
İrini

Soğukçeşme
Sokak

Imperial
Gate

Carpet
Museum

Fountain of

Taya Hatun Sk

Istasyon Arkası Sk

Nöbethane Cad

Hüdavendigar Cad

İbn-i Kemal Cad

Ebussuud Cad

Hocapaşa Sk

Gülhane

Alayköşkü Cad

Hükümet Konağı Cad

Salkım Söğüt Sk

Caferağa
Medresesi

Soğukçeşme Sk

Caferiye Sk

Alemdar Cad

Yerebatan Cad

SİRKECİ

Sirkeci

Muradiye
Cad

Ankara Cad

Sirkeci

EMİNÖNÜ

Hamidiye Cad

Yalı Köşkü Cad

Büyük Postane Cad

Aşir Efendi Cad

Köprücü Sk

HOBYAR

Cemal Nadir Sk

Hoca Hani Sk

Celal Ferdi
Gökçay Sk

Tasvir Sk

Ankara Cad

Cağaloğlu Yokuşu

CAĞALOĞLU

Şeref Efendi Sk

Cağaloğlu
Meydanı

Tasçılar Sk

Prof Kazım İsmail Gürkan
Cad

Molla Feneri Sk

ALEMDAR

Ticarethane Sk

Sultanahmet

Nuruosmaniye Cad

Bab-ı Ali Cad

Türbedar Sk

Çatal Çeşme Cad

Divan Yolu Cad

For reviews see	
⊙ Top Sights	p44
⊙ Sights	p51
✕ Eating	p53
🍷 Drinking	p56
✪ Entertainment	p57
🛍 Shopping	p57

200 m
0.1 miles

N

SAIKO3P/SHUTTERSTOCK ©

Carpet Museum

Sights

Carpet Museum
MUSEUM

1 ⊙ Map p50, D4

Housed in an *imaret* (soup kitchen) added to the Aya Sofya complex in the 18th century, this museum is entered through a spectacular baroque gate and gives the visitor an excellent overview of the history of Anatolian carpet making. The carpets, which have been sourced from mosques throughout the country, date from the 14th to 20th centuries. (Halı Müzesi; ☏0212-518 1330; www.halimuzesi.com; cnr Babıhümayun Caddesi & Soğukçeşme Sokak; admission ₺10; ⊙9am-6pm Tue-Sun mid-Apr–mid-Oct, to 4pm mid-Oct–mid-Apr; ⛢Sultanahmet or Gülhane)

Aya İrini
CHURCH

2 ⊙ Map p50, C4

Commissioned by Justinian in the 540s, this Byzantine church is almost exactly as old as its near neighbour, Aya Sofya. Used as an arsenal for centuries, it is now open to visitors but the entrance fee is exorbitant considering the fact that there are no exhibits inside. (Hagia Eirene, Church of the Divine Peace; ☏0212-512 0480; http://topkapisarayi.gov.tr/en/hagia-irene-0; 1st Court, Topkapı Palace; adult/child under 6yr ₺20/free; ⊙9am-7pm Wed-Mon Apr–mid-Oct, to 5pm mid-Oct–Mar; ⛢Sultanahmet)

Gülhane Park

PARK

3 ◉ Map p50, C2

Gülhane Park was once the outer garden of Topkapı Palace, accessible only to the royal court. These days crowds of locals come here to picnic under the many trees, promenade past the formally planted flowerbeds, and enjoy wonderful views of the Bosphorus, Sea of Marmara and Princes' Islands from the **Set Üstü Çay Bahçesi** (◷7am-10pm; pot of çay ₺10, snacks ₺3 to ₺10) on the park's northeastern edge. The park is especially lovely during the **İstanbul Tulip Festival** (admission free; ◷April), when tulips are arranged to resemble *nazar boncuk* 'evil eye' charms. (Gülhane Parkı; ◷7am-10pm; 🚇Gülhane)

Ahmet Hamdi Tanpınar Literature Museum Library

LIBRARY

4 ◉ Map p50, C3

Built into the wall of Gülhane Park, the Alay Köşkü (Parade Kiosk) is where the sultan would sit and watch the periodic parades of troops and trade guilds that commemorated great holidays and military victories. It is now open to the public as a literature museum and library named in honour of novelist and essayist Ahmet Hamdi Tanpınar (1901–62). (Ahmet Hamdi Tanpınar Edebiyat Müze Kütüphanesi; 📞0212-520 2081; Gülhane Park; admission free; ◷10am-7pm Mon-Sat; 🚇Gülhane)

İstanbul Museum of the History of Science & Technology in Islam

MUSEUM

5 ◉ Map p50, C2

Of interest to science buffs, the didactic exhibition in this museum argues that Islamic advances in science and technology preceded and greatly influenced those in Europe. Most of the exhibits are reconstructions of historical instruments and tools used by astronomers, seafarers and others. (İstanbul İslam Bilim ve Teknoloji Tarihi Müzesi; 📞0212-528 8065; www.ibttm.org; Has Ahırlar Binaları, Gülhane Park; adult/child under 12yr ₺10/free; ◷9am-6.30pm Wed-Mon mid-Apr–Oct, to 4.30pm Nov–mid-Apr, last entry 30min before closing; 🚇Gülhane)

Soğukçeşme Sokak

HISTORIC SITE

6 ◉ Map p50, C4

Running between the Topkapı Palace walls and Aya Sofya, this picturesque cobbled street is named after the Soğuk Çeşme (Cold Fountain) at its southern end. It is home to the Carpet Museum, to a row of faux-Ottoman houses functioning as a hotel and to an undoubtedly authentic restored Byzantine cistern that now operates as the hotel restaurant. (🚇Sultanahmet or Gülhane)

ULITA KRAKOS/SHUTTERSTOCK ©

Exhibit at the Museum of the History of Science & Technology in Islam, Gülhane Park

Caferağa Medresesi

HISTORIC BUILDING

7 ⊙ Map p50, C4

This lovely little building tucked away in the shadow of Aya Sofya was designed by Ottoman architect Mimar Sinan on the orders of Cafer Ağa, Süleyman the Magnificent's chief black eunuch. Built in 1560 as a school, it now houses a cultural organisation that teaches and promotes traditional Turkish handicrafts. The courtyard is home to the pleasant Caferağa Medresesi Çay Bahçesi (p56) tea garden. (☏0212-513 3601; www.tkhv.org; Soğukkuyu Çıkmazı 5, off Caferiye Sokak; admission free; ⊗9am-7pm Tue-Sun; ⛴Sultanahmet)

Eating

Matbah

OTTOMAN €€€

9 ✕ Map p50, C4

One of a growing number of İstanbul restaurants specialising in so-called Ottoman palace cuisine, Matbah offers dishes that were devised centuries ago in the royal kitchens of Constantinople. The menu changes with the season and features unusual ingredients such as goose, quail, quince and molasses. Try the sailor's roll starter (seven cheeses wrapped in filo, fried and drizzled with honey). (☏0212-514 6151; www.matbahrestaurant. com; Ottoman Hotel Imperial, Caferiye Sokak

Understand

The Ottoman Empire

Rise of a Dynasty

In the 13th century, a Turkish warlord named Osman (b 1258), known as Gazi (Warrior for the Faith), inherited a small territory from his warlord father. Osman's followers became known as Osmanlıs (Ottomans).

Osman died in 1324. His son Orhan captured Bursa from the Byzantines in 1324, made it his base and declared himself sultan of the Ottoman Empire. Thessaloniki was captured from the Venetians in 1387 and Kosovo from the Serbs in 1389, marking the start of the Ottoman expansion into Europe. Soon, the acquisition of the great city of Constantinople and control of the overland trade routes between Europe and Asia became the dynasty's major objective.

In 1451, 21-year-old Mehmet II became sultan. On 29 May 1453 his army breached Constantinople's massive land walls and took control of the city, bringing the Byzantine Empire to an end. Mehmet was given the title Fatih (Conqueror) and began to rebuild and repopulate the city.

Mehmet died in 1481, but the building boom he kicked off was continued by worthy successors including Sultan Selim I (r 1512–20) and Sultan Süleyman I (r 1520–66), known as 'the Magnificent'.

Decline & Fall

After Süleyman's death, the power of the empire slowly disintegrated. In 1683 the Ottoman army was defeated by the Holy Roman Empire at the Battle of Vienna, marking the end of both its military supremacy and the Ottoman expansion into Europe.

A series of incompetent sultans further weakened the empire. There were some exceptions – Selim III (r 1789–1807), who unsuccessfully attempted to modernise the army, and Mahmut II (r 1808–39), who was finally successful in this aim – but they were few and far between. The 19th-century Tanzimat political reforms ushered in by Mahmut II and continued by Abdülmecid I (r 1839–61) took some strides towards modernity, but it was not enough to save the sultanate, which was abolished in 1922. The last of the Osmanlıs to rule as sultan, Mehmet VI (r 1918–22), was expelled from Turkey at this time, and Mustafa Kemal Atatürk became president of the new Turkish Republic.

Lokum (Turkish Delight)

6/1; mezes ₺15-23, mains ₺29-61; ☻noon-
10.30pm; 🛜✍; 🚇Sultanahmet)

Sefa Restaurant TURKISH €

8 🍴 Map p50, A4

Describing its cuisine as Ottoman,
this popular place offers *hazır yemek*
(ready-made dishes) and kebaps at
reasonable prices. You can order from
an English menu, but at busy times
you may find it easier to just pick
daily specials from the bain-marie.
Try to arrive early-ish for lunch because many dishes run out by 1.30pm.
No alcohol. (☎0212-520 0670; www.
sefarestaurant.com.tr; Nuruosmaniye Caddesi

11, Cağaloğlu; portions ₺8-14, kebaps ₺20;
☻7am-5pm; ✍; 🚇Sultanahmet)

Gülhane Kandil Tesisleri TURKISH €

11 🍴 Map p50, C2

In spring, the perfume from a
profusion of hyacinths blooming in
Gülhane Park wafts over the outdoor
tables of this garden cafe, which is
built into the park's historic walls.
It's a lovely spot, when the weather is
kind, for breakfast, a light lunch
or a coffee break; Turkish coffee ₺5,
çay ₺2.50. (☎0212-444 6644; www.
beltur.istanbul; Gülhane Park; sandwiches

₺6.50-16.50, all-day breakfast plates ₺22, mains ₺19; ⊙11am-10pm; 🚇Gülhane)

Güvenç Konyalı   TURKISH €€

10 🍴 Map p50, B2

Specialities from Konya in Central Anatolia are the draw at this bustling place just off the much-loved Hocapaşa Sokak food strip. Regulars come for the spicy *bamya çorbası* (sour soup with lamb and chickpeas), *etli ekmek* (flat bread with meat) and meltingly soft slow-cooked meats from the oven. No alcohol. (📞0212-

Local Life
Hocapaşa Sokak

If you're in the Sirkeci neighbourhood at lunchtime, join the locals in this pedestrianised street lined with cheap eateries. Here, an array of *lokantas* serve *hazır yemek* (ready-made dishes) from steaming bain-maries and a variety of kebab and köfte joints do a bustling takeaway trade. The oldest business on the street, tiny **Hocapaşa Pidecisi** (📞0212-512 0990; www.hocapasa.com. tr; Hocapaşa Sokak 19, Sirkeci; pides ₺8-20; ⊙noon-8pm; 🚇Sirkeci) has been serving piping-hot pides (Turkish-style pizzas) straight from the oven since 1964 and remains as popular as ever.

527 5220; Hocapaşa Hamam Sokak 4, Sirkeci; soups ₺6-10, mains & pides ₺15-25; ⊙11.30am-9pm; 🚇Sirkeci)

Hafız Mustafa   SWEETS €

12 🍴 Map p50, B2

Making locals happy since 1864, this *şekerlemeleri* (sweets shop) sells *lokum* (Turkish Delight), milk puddings and spinach or cheese *börek* (filled pastry). Put your sweet tooth to good use in the upstairs cafe, or choose a selection of indulgences to take home (you might want to avoid the baklava, though, which isn't the best). (📞0212-527 6654; www. hafizmustafa.com; Muradiye Caddesi 51, Sirkeci; börek ₺5, baklava ₺6-7.50, puddings ₺6; ⊙9am-6pm; 🛜; 🚇Sirkeci)

Drinking

Caferağa Medresesi Çay Bahçesi   TEA GARDEN

On a fine day, sipping a *çay* in the gorgeous courtyard of this Sinan-designed *medrese* (see 7 ◉ Map p50, C4), is a delight. Located close to both Aya Sofya and Topkapı Palace, it houses a craft centre and serves simple food at lunchtime. (📞0212-513 3601; www.tkhv. org; Soğukkuyu Çıkmazı 5, off Caferiye Sokak; ⊙9am-7pm Tue-Sun; 🚇Sultanahmet)

Entertainment

Hodjapasha Cultural Centre
PERFORMING ARTS

13 ⭐ Map p50, B2

Occupying a beautifully converted 550-year-old hamam, this cultural centre stages a one-hour whirling-dervish performance at 7pm on Tuesday, Thursday and Saturday year-round, with additional performances in busy months (daily in April, May, September and October). Note that children under seven are not admitted; and switch off your phone, as readers have reported draconian crowd-control here. (📞0212-511 4626; www.hodjapasha.com; Hocapaşa Hamamı Sokak 3b, Sirkeci; performances adult ₺70-80, child under 12yr ₺40-50; 🚊Sirkeci)

Shopping

Özlem Tuna
JEWELLERY, HOMEWARES

14 🔒 Map p50, B1

A leader in Turkey's contemporary design movement, Özlem Tuna produces super-stylish jewellery and homewares and sells them from her atelier overlooking Sirkeci train station. Her pieces use forms and colours that reference İstanbul's history and culture (tulips, seagulls, Byzantine mosaics, *nazar boncuk* 'evil eye' charms) and include hamam bowls, coffee and teasets, coasters, rings, earrings, cufflinks and necklaces. (📞0212-527 9285; www.ozlemtuna.com; 5th fl, Nemlizade Han, Ankara Caddesi 65, Eminönü; 🕘9am-6pm Mon-Fri; 🚊Sirkeci)

Ali Muhiddin Hacı Bekir
FOOD

15 🔒 Map p50, A1

Many people think that this historic shop, which has been operated by members of the same family for over 200 years, is the best place in the city to buy *lokum* (Turkish Delight). With other **branches** in Beyoğlu (📞0212-244 2804; İstiklal Caddesi 83; Ⓜ Taksim) and Kadıköy (📞0216-336 1519; Muvakkithane Caddesi 6; 🕘8am-8pm; 🚢Kadıköy), customers can choose from *sade* (plain), *cevizli* (walnut), *fıstıklı* (pistachio), *badem* (almond) or *roze* (rose water). (📞0212-522 8543; www.hacibekir.com.tr; Hamidiye Caddesi 33, Eminönü; 🕘9am-7.30pm; 🚊Eminönü)

Explore

Grand Bazaar & the Bazaar District

Crowned by the historic Grand Bazaar (Kapalı Çarşı; pictured), this beguiling neighbourhood is also home to the smaller but equally historic Spice Bazaar (Mısır Çarşısı), the upmarket shopping street of Nuruosmaniye Caddesi and the frantically busy shopping precinct around Mahmutpaşa Yokuşu. Presiding over the mercantile mayhem is the Süleymaniye, İstanbul's most magnificent Ottoman mosque.

The Sights in a Day

☀️ The **Grand Bazaar** (p60) is best visited in the morning, when shopkeepers enjoy gossiping with their neighbours over a glass of tea and are less likely to hassle prospective customers. Wander through this ancient shopping mall for two or three hours, stopping for a coffee or tea at one of its cafes before enjoying lunch at one of its many *kebabçıs* (kebap eateries).

☀️ Visit the **Süleymaniye Mosque** (p64), take a break at **Lale Bahçesi** (p76) or the **Mimar Sinan Teras Cafe** (p76), and then walk down the hill towards the **Spice Bazaar** (p70), popping into the **Rüstem Paşa Mosque** (p67) on the way and the **New Mosque** (p70) and **Hünkâr Kasrı** (p70) afterwards.

🌙 **Siirt Şeref Büryan Kebap** (p73) and **Sur Ocakbaşı** (p73) in the Kadınlar Pazarı (Women's Market) in Zeyrek are great choices for a frills-free dinner. For something more sophisticated, head to the panoramic terrace floor of **Hamdi Restaurant** (p72) in Eminönü.

For a local's day in the Bazaar District, see p66.

👁 Top Sights

Grand Bazaar (p60)

Süleymaniye Mosque (p64)

🔍 Local Life

Between the Bazaars (p66)

❤️ Best of İstanbul

Shopping

Abdulla Natural Products (p77)

Necef Antik & Gold (p77)

Altan Şekerleme (p77)

Ümit Berksoy (p78)

Yazmacı Necdet Danış (p78)

Derviş (p77)

Çay Bahçesis

Erenler Nargile ve Çay Bahçesi (p76)

Lale Bahçesi (p76)

Getting There

Ⓜ **Metro** From Beyoğlu, take the Yenikapı service and alight at Haliç for the Spice Bazaar and Vezneciler for the Grand Bazaar and Süleymaniye Mosque.

🚋 **Tram** Alight at Beyazıt-Kapalı Çarşı for the Grand Bazaar, Eminönü for the Spice Bazaar and Laleli-Üniversite for the Süleymaniye Mosque.

Top Sights
Grand Bazaar

When Mehmet the Conqueror laid the Kapalı Çarşı's foundation stone in 1455, he gave the imperial imprimatur to a local mercantile tradition that has remained strong ever since. Located in the centre of the Old City, this atmospheric covered market is the heart of İstanbul in much more than a geographic sense – artisans learn their trade here, businessmen negotiate important deals and tourists make a valuable contribution to the local economy (occasionally, it must be said, against their better judgements).

Kapalı Çarşı, Covered Market

👁 Map p68, F4

www.kapalicarsi.org.tr

🕗8.30am-7pm Mon-Sat, last entry 6pm

🚊Beyazıt Kapalıçarşı

Nuruosmaniye Mosque & Gate
Built in Ottoman baroque style between 1748 and 1755, this **mosque** (Nuruosmaniye Camii, Light of Osman Mosque; Map p62; Vezir Han Caddesi, Beyazıt; 🚊Çemberlitaş) is on the busy pedestrian route from Cağaloğlu Meydanı and Nuruosmaniye Caddesi to the bazaar and has an unusual polygonal rear courtyard. It stands next to one of the major entrances to the Grand Bazaar, the Nuruosmaniye Kapısı (Nuruosmaniye Gate), which is adorned with a golden *tuğra* (crest of the sultan).

Kalpakçılar Caddesi
Shop windows crammed with glittering gold jewellery line both sides of the bazaar's busiest thoroughfare. Originally named after the makers of *kalpakçılars* (fur hats) who had their stores here, it's now full of jewellers who pay up to US$90,000 per year in rent for this high-profile location. In recent years chain retail stores have begun to open outlets along its length, triggering protests by the bazaar's traditional artisans.

Sandal Bedestenı
Undergoing a major restoration when this book went to print, this 16th-century stone warehouse featuring 20 small domes was built during the reign of Süleyman the Magnificent and is named after the *sandal* (fabric woven with silk) that was sold and stored here.

İç (Inner) Bedesten
Also known as the Eski (Old) Bedesten, this is the oldest part of the bazaar and has always been an area where precious items are stored and sold. These days it's where most of the bazaar's antique stores are located. Also here are top-quality jewellers such as Necef Antik & Gold (p77) and Ümit Berksoy (p78).

☑ Top Tips
▶ To visit ateliers where traditional artisans work, sign up for the Grand Bazaar Walk conducted by İstanbul Walks (www.istanbulwalks.com).

▶ Alternative City Tours (www.alternativecitytours.com) runs specialist photographic tours and a kids' scavenger hunt in the bazaar.

▶ Bargaining is an accepted practice in traditional carpet, antique and jewellery shops, but the chic homewares shops have fixed prices.

✕ Take a Break
Cafes are scattered throughout the bazaar. Our favourites include Şark Kahvesi (p76) and Ethem Tezçakar Kahveci (p76).

For a cheap and tasty lunch, head to Aynen Dürüm (p74) just inside the Kılıççılar Gate or Dürümcü Raif Usta (p74) near the corner of Kılıççılar Sokak and Küçük Yıldız Han Sokak.

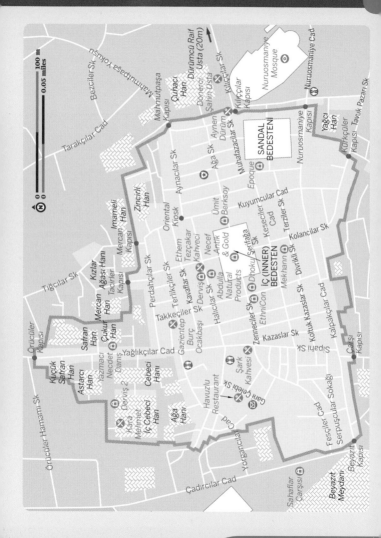

Halıcılar Çarşışı Sokak

The most photogenic street in the bazaar is also the most enticing. Home to designer stores such as Abdulla Natural Products (p77) and Derviş (p77), it also has a number of popular cafes.

Kuyumcular Caddesi

The name of this street pays tribute to the *kuyumcular* (jewellers) who have always been based here; these days it's the centre of the bazaar's silver merchants. Also here is one of the bazaar's most unusual features, a quaint 19th-century timber structure known as the Oriental Kiosk. Once home to the most famous *muhallebici* (milk pudding shop) in the district, it now functions as a jewellery store.

Zincirli Han

Accessed off Kuyumcular Caddesi and named after the *zincirli* (chains) that were once manufactured here, this pretty cobbled caravanserai is now home to one of the bazaar's best-known carpet merchants.

Tekkeçiler Sokak

This charming street was named after the *tekkeçilers* (skullcap makers) who once plied their trade here. It's now known for its marble *sebils* (public drinking fountains) and shops selling kilims (pileless woven rugs). These include designer stores such as Dhoku (p78), which offers kilims featuring modern and avant-garde designs.

Textile Stores

Many of the best textile stores in İstanbul are located on or near the bazaar's major north–south axis – Sipahi Sokak and Yağlıkçılar Caddesi. The crush of shoppers here can occasionally resemble a cavalry charge (in Turkish, *sipahi* means 'cavalry soldier'), but it's worth braving the crowds to visit famous stores such as Yazmacı Necdet Danış (p78), which sells a wonderful array of fabrics.

İç Cebeci Han

This is one of the largest of the bazaar's many caravanserais. In Ottoman times it would have offered travelling merchants accommodation and a place to do business; these days it's home to artisans' workshops, a branch of the Derviş (p77) bathwares shop and a popular *kebapçı* (kebap eatery) called Kara Mehmet.

Sahaflar Çarşısı

The 'Secondhand Book Bazaar' has operated as a book and paper market since Byzantine times. At the centre of its shady courtyard is a bust of İbrahim Müteferrika (1674–1745), who printed the first book in Turkey in 1732.

Top Sights
Süleymaniye Mosque

Commissioned by Süleyman the Magnificent in 1550, the Süleymaniye was the fourth imperial mosque built in İstanbul and it certainly lives up to its patron's nickname. Crowning one of İstanbul's seven hills, it's the Old City's major landmark and the spiritual hub of the Bazaar District. Though not the largest of the city's Ottoman-era mosques, it is unusual in that many of its original *külliye* (mosque complex) buildings have been retained and sympathetically adapted for reuse.

👁 Map p68, E2

Professor Sıddık Sami Onar Caddesi

Ⓜ Vezneciler

Interior

Minarets

The four minarets with their 10 beautiful *şerefes* (balconies) are said to represent the fact that Süleyman was the fourth of the Ottoman sultans to rule the city and the 10th sultan after the establishment of the empire.

Interior

The mosque's architect, Mimar Sinan, incorporated four buttresses into the walls of the building – the result is open, airy and highly reminiscent of Aya Sofya, especially as the dome is nearly as large as the one crowning the great Byzantine basilica. Also notable is the *mihrab* (prayer niche indicating the direction of Mecca), which is decorated with fine İznik tiles.

Tombs

To the right (southeast) of the main entrance is the cemetery, home to the *türbes* (tombs) of Süleyman and his wife Haseki Hürrem Sultan (Roxelana). The tilework in both is superb, as are the ivory-inlaid panels in Süleyman's tomb.

İmaret

The mosque's *imaret* (soup kitchen) is on its northwestern edge and its tranquil courtyard is a lovely place to enjoy a çay.

Tiryaki Çarşısı

The street facing the mosque's main entrance is now called Professor Sıddık Sami Onar Caddesi, but was formerly known as the Tiryaki Çarşısı (Market of the Addicts) as it was home to teahouses selling opium. These now house popular *fasülye* (bean) restaurants including Kuru Fasulyeci Erzincanlı Ali Baba (p74).

☑ Top Tips

▶ In the garden behind the mosque is a terrace with lovely views of the Golden Horn (Haliç).

▶ The surrounding streets are home to many Ottoman timber houses. To see some, head down Fetva Yokuşu and then veer right into Namahrem Sokak and into Ayrancı Sokak.

▶ Visitors to the mosque must remove their shoes; women should cover their heads with a scarf or shawl.

▶ Avoid visiting at lunchtime on Friday, when weekly sermons and group prayers are held.

✕ Take a Break

For an unusual pick-me-up, head down the streets southwest of the mosque to sample *boza* at historic Vefa Bozacısı (p76).

The panoramic terrace of the Mimar Sinan Teras Cafe (p76), located in the street beneath the mosque, is a great choice for a çay break.

Local Life
Between the Bazaars

Locals outnumber tourists by a generous margin in the crowded and cacophanous streets surrounding the Grand and Spice Bazaars. Here, housewives source bargains, street vendors hawk fresh fruit and pastries, and the atmosphere crackles with good-humoured energy.

❶ Mahmutpaşa Kapısı
Exit the Grand Bazaar by gate 18 and you'll find yourself on the busy thoroughfare of Mahmutpaşa Yokuşu, which runs down to the Spice Bazaar and is home to shops selling everything from coffee cups to circumcision outfits.

❷ Kılıççılar Sokak
Running east from the bazaar's Kılıççılar Kapısı (Kılıççılar Gate), this narrow street behind the Nuruosmaniye Mosque is replete with stands selling traditional snacks such as

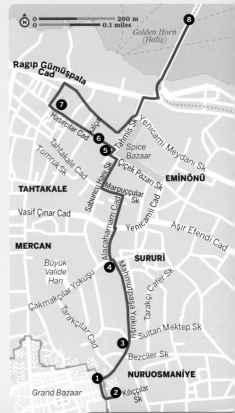

döner kebap (spit-roasted lamb) and *kokoreç* (seasoned lamb or mutton intestines wrapped around a skewer and grilled over charcoal) to the bazaar's shopkeepers, artisans and porters.

❸ Mahmutpaşa Hamamı

One of the oldest Ottoman hamams in the city (it dates from 1476), this **building** (Mahmutpaşa Yokuşu; 🚇Çemberlitaş) was converted into a downmarket shopping centre a decade or so ago. Its domed ceiling, stained-glass windows and marble floor offer a glimpse of its former glory.

❹ Islamic Chic

In Bebek and Beyoğlu the fashion might be for tight jeans, revealing jackets and chunky jewellery, but here in the Old City there's little make-up and even less flesh on show. Wildly popular clothing chain store **Armine** (✆0212-511 2211; www.armine.com; Mahmutpaşa Yokuşu 135, Eminönü; ⏱10am-6pm Mon-Sat; 🚇Eminönü) is where Zara style meets the headscarf.

❺ Turkish Coffee to Take Home

Tahmis Sokak on the western edge of the Spice Bazaar hosts a jumble of stalls selling slabs of pungent farmhouse cheese, tubs of olives and mounds of *biber salçası* (hot pepper paste). Also here is the flagship store of Turkey's most famous coffee purveyor, **Kurukahveci Mehmet Efendi** (✆0212-511 4262; www.mehmetefendi.com; Tahmis Sokak 66, Eminönü; ⏱8am-8pm Mon-Sat; 🚇Eminönü).

❻ Hasırcılar Caddesi

The shops lining this narrow street running parallel to the Golden Horn sell everything from teapots to toothbrushes. Stock up on provisions or pop into **Develi Baklava** (✆0212-512 1261; Hasırcılar Caddesi 89, Eminönü; portions ₺10-12; ⏱7am-7pm Mon-Sat; 🚇Eminönü) to sample what may well be İstanbul's most delicious sweet treat.

❼ Rüstem Paşa Mosque

This diminutive **mosque** (Rüstem Paşa Camii; Hasırcılar Caddesi, Rüstem Paşa; 🚇Eminönü) is a gem. Dating from 1560, it was designed by Mimar Sinan for Rüstem Paşa, son-in-law and grand vizier of Süleyman the Magnificent. A showpiece of the best Ottoman architecture and tilework, it's accessed via stairs off Hasırcılar Caddesi or from a side street to the right (north). Avoid visiting during prayer times, when local shopkeepers worship here.

❽ Galata Bridge

This İstanbul **icon** (Galata Köprüsü; 🚇Eminönü, Karaköy) carries a constant flow of locals crossing between Beyoğlu and Eminönü, hopeful anglers trailing their lines into the waters below, and a continually changing procession of street vendors hawking everything from fresh-baked *simits* (sesame-encrusted bread rings) to Rolex rip-offs. Consider enjoying a beer and nargile (water pipe) in one of the lower-level cafes while watching the ferries ply the surrounding waters.

Çırçır Cad

İbadethane Sk

8 Church of the Monastery of Christ Pantokrator

Tetimmeler Cad

Zeyrek Cad

Atpazar Sk

Eski Mutaflar Sk

ZEYREK

Melekşah Sk

Tavanlı Çeşme Sk

Hızır Külhanı Sk

VEFA

Şemsettin Sk

İmam Niyazi Sk

Kırbacı Sk

İtfaiye Cad

Kendir Sk

Atatürk Bul

İmaret Sabunhan

Katip Çelebi Sk

Azep Askeri Sk

Darülhadis Sk

Vefa Türbesi Sk

Şair Beyazıt Cad

Vefa Cad

Oluk Sk

20 Şifa

Prof Ona

Sami Ona

Cad

Suyolu Sk

Tezgâhçılar Sk

Ömerefendi

12 11 Women's Bazaar

Revani Çelebi Sk

Himmet Sk

Molla Şemsettin Cami Sk

Yoğurtçuoğlu Sk

15

Ayşekadın Hamamı

9

Macar Kardeşler Cad

Fatih İtfaiye Park

İtfaiye Cad

7 Aqueduct of Valens

Fatih Anıt Park

Cemal Yener Tosyalı Sk

Islah Sk

23

Vefa Cad

MOLLA HÜSREV

Horhor Cad

SARAÇHANE

Saraçhane Park

KALENDERHANE

Şehzade Mehmet 4 Mosque

Dede Efendi Cad

Taştekneler Sk

Kazlı Mescit Sk

Cüce Çeşmesi Sk

Delikanlı Sk

Bozdoğan Kemeri Cad

Süleymaniye Cad

Besim Ömer Paşa Ca

Darülhan Cad

Darülelhan Şehitleri Cad

Şehzadebaşı Cad

Atatürk Bul

Gençtürk Cad

Fevziye Cad

BALABAN AĞA

Vezneciler

16 Mart Şehitleri Cad

Vezneciler Cad

Ağa Yokuşu Sk

Vidinli Tefikpaşa Cad

Büyük Reşit Paşa Cad

Çukur Çeşme Sk

Fethibey Cad

Zeynep Kamil Sk

0   200 m
0   0.1 miles

Kurultay Sk

LALELİ

Laleli-Üniversite

Laleli Cad

Ordu Cad

Şair Fitnat Sk

Ağa Çeşmesi Sk

Şair Haşmet Sk

RÜSTEMPAŞA

Kible Çeşme Cad
Ragıp Gümüşpala Cad
26

E **F** **G** **H**

hayriye Hanım Sk

Galata Bridge
(Galata Köprüsü)

1

EMİRTAŞ

Resadiye Cad

Kutucular Cad

Fetva Yokuşu

Mimar Sinan Cad

Prof Cemil Birsel Cad

Siyavuşpaşa Sk

Dökmeciler Hamamı Sk

Tahtakale Cad

Tomruk Sk

Uzunçarşı Cad

Kalçın Sk
10

Yenicami Meydanı Sk
New
Mosque
1
Spice
Bazaar
2
3 Hünkâr
Kasrı

Eminönü

2

Çiçek Pazarı Sk

**leymaniye
Mosque**

Şahande Sk

Vasıf Çınar Cad

TAHTAKALE

Sabuncu Hanı Sk

Marpuççular Sk

Yenicami Cad

EMİNÖNÜ

Hamidiye Cad

Büyük Postane Cad

Prof Sıddık Sami
Onar Cad

Havancı Sk

MERCAN

Nargileci Sk

Alacahamam Cad

Aşir Efendi Cad

Hanımeli Sk

HOBYAR

Cemal Nadir Sk

3

**İstanbul
University**

Semaver Sk

Furat Paşa Cad

Mercan Cad

Çakmakçılar Yokuşu

Tarakçılar Cad

Tarakçılar Sk

Çarkçılar Sk

SURURİ

Mahmutpaşa Yokuşu

Tarakçı Cafer Sk

Çeşnici Sk

Sultan Mektep Sk

Hoca Hanı Sk

Türkocağı Cad

Tığcılar Sk

Yağlıkçılar Cad

29

Halıcılar Sk

16
27 21 24
22 31
18 30 28
32
Fesçiler Cad
Kalpakçılar Cad

Grand Bazaar

Çadırcılar Cad

25

Bezciler Sk

17
13

NURUOSMANİYE

14

Kılıçcılar Sk

Nuruosmaniye Sk

Kuyumcular Cad

Mengene Sk

Şeref Efendi Sk

Tasvir Sk

Nuruosmaniye Cad

4

33

Türbedar Sk

Bab-ı Ali Cad

5 Beyazıt
Square

BEYAZIT

Beyazıt
Kapalıçarşı

Çarşıkapı Cad

19

Tavuk Pazarı Sk

Bileyciler Sk

Kürkçüler Pazarı Sk

ÇEMBERLİTAŞ

6 Column of
Constantine

5

Mithatpaşa Cad

Asma Kandil Sk

Divan Yolu Cad

Çemberlitaş

Sights

Spice Bazaar
MARKET

1 ◉ Map p68, G2

Vividly coloured spices are displayed alongside jewel-like *lokum* (Turkish Delight) at this Ottoman-era marketplace, providing eye candy for the thousands of tourists and locals who make their way here every day. Stalls also sell caviar, dried herbs, honey, nuts and dried fruits. The number of stalls selling tourist trinkets increases annually, yet this remains a great place to stock up on edible souvenirs, share a few jokes with vendors and marvel at the well-preserved building. (Mısır Çarşısı, Egyptian Market; ☏212-513 6597; www.misircarsisi.org; ⊙8am-7.30pm; ⊠Eminönü)

New Mosque
MOSQUE

2 ◉ Map p68, H2

Only in İstanbul would a 400-year-old mosque be called 'new'. Constructed between 1597 and 1665, its design references both the Blue Mosque and the Süleymaniye Mosque, with a large forecourt and a square sanctuary surmounted by a series of semidomes crowned by a grand dome. The interior is richly decorated with gold leaf, İznik tiles and carved marble. (Yeni Camii; Yenicamii Meydanı Sokak, Eminönü; ⊠Eminönü)

Hünkâr Kasrı
MUSEUM

3 ◉ Map p68, H2

Built over a grand archway attached to the New Mosque, this small *kasrı*

(pavilion) or *mahfili* (loge), dates from the same period and functioned as a waiting area and retreat for the sultans. It comprises a salon, bedchamber and toilet and is decorated with exquisite İznik tiles throughout. Entry is via an extremely long and wide staircase that is now ulitised by the İstanbul Ticaret Odası (Chamber of Commerce) as a temporary exhibition space. (Hünkâr Mahfili; Arpacılar Caddesi 29, Eminönü; admission free; ⊙9am-5pm Mon-Sat during exhibitions; ⊠Eminönü)

Şehzade Mehmet Mosque
MOSQUE

4 ◉ Map p68, B3

Süleyman the Magnificent built this square-shaped mosque between 1543 and 1548 as a memorial to his son Mehmet, who died of smallpox in 1543 at the age of 22. It was the first important mosque to be designed by Mimar Sinan and has a lovely garden setting, two double-balconied minarets and attractive exterior decoration. Inside, the central dome is supported by four semidomes (one on each side of the square). (Şehzade Mehmet Camii, Mosque of the Prince; Şehzadebaşı Caddesi, Kalenderhane; Ⓜ Vezneciler)

Beyazıt Square
SQUARE

5 ◉ Map p68, E5

In Byzantine times, this public square was called the Forum of Theodosius. Today it's home to street vendors, students from the adjoining **İstanbul University** (⊠Laleli-Üniversite) and plenty of pigeons. The main building here is the **Beyazıt Mosque** (Beyazıt Camii, Mosque of Sultan Beyazıt II; 🚋Beyazıt-Kapalı Çarşı), and there are also various buildings that originally formed part of its *külliye*. These include a *medrese* that now houses a Museum of Calligraphy (currently closed for restoration); an *imaret* (soup kitchen) and *kervansaray* (caravanserai) complex now functioning as the magnificent Beyazıt State Library; and a disused double hamam. (Beyazıt Meydanı, Hürriyet (Freedom) Meydanı; 🚋Beyazıt-Kapalı Çarşı)

Column of Constantine

MONUMENT

6 ◉ Map p68, G5

Erected by order of the Emperor Constantine to celebrate the dedication of New Rome (Constantinople) as capital of the Roman Empire in 330, this column is one of the city's most ancient monuments. Located in a pigeon-packed plaza next to the Çemberlitaş tram stop, it once stood in the grand Forum of Constantine and was topped by a statue of the great emperor himself in the guise of Apollo. (Hooped Column; Divan Yolu Caddesi, Çemberlitaş; 🚋Çemberlitaş)

Aqueduct of Valens

LANDMARK

7 ◉ Map p68, B2

Rising majestically over the traffic on busy Atatürk Bulvarı, this limestone

aqueduct is one of the city's most distinctive landmarks. Commissioned by the Emperor Valens and completed in AD 378, it linked the third and fourth hills and carried water to a cistern at Beyazıt Meydanı before finally ending up at the Great Palace of Byzantium.

The aqueduct was part of an elaborate system sourcing water from the north of the city and linking more than 250km of water channels, some 30 bridges and more than 100 cisterns within the city walls, making it one of the greatest hydraulic engineering achievements of ancient times. After the Conquest, it supplied the Eski (Old) and Topkapı Palaces with water. (Atatürk Bulvarı, Zeyrek; Ⓜ Vezneciler)

Church of the Monastery of Christ Pantokrator

MONASTERY

8 Map p68, B1

This church and a series of cisterns are the only remaining structures of an important Byzantine monastery complex that also included a library, hospital and chapel. One of the finest examples of Byzantine architecture in İstanbul, it is the second-largest surviving Byzantine church in the city after Aya Sofya. Sorely neglected for centuries, it is currently undergoing a controversial restoration. (Molla Zeyrek Camii; İbadethane Sokak, Zeyrek; MVezneciler)

Eating

Fatih Damak Pide

PIDE €

9 Map p68, A2

It's worth making the trek to this *pideci* overlooking the Fatih İtfaiye Park near the Aqueduct of Valens. Its reputation for making the best Karadeniz (Black Sea)–style pide on the historic peninsula is well deserved and the pots of tea served with meals are a nice touch (the first pot is free, subsequent pots are charged). (☎0212-521 5057; www.fatihdamakpide.com; Büyük Karaman Caddesi 48, Fatih; pides ₺17-25; ⏰7am-11pm; MVezneciler)

Hamdi Restaurant

KEBAP €€

10 Map p68, G2

One of the city's best-loved restaurants, this place near the Spice Bazaar is owned by Hamdi Arpacı, who started out as a street-food vendor in the 1960s. His tasty Urfa-style kebaps were so popular that he soon graduated from his modest stand to this building, which has views of the Old City, Golden Horn and Galata from its top-floor terrace. (☎0212-444 6463; www.hamdirestorant.com.tr; Kalçın Sokak 11, Eminönü; mezes ₺11.50-26, kebaps ₺28-50; ⏰noon-midnight; P❄♿; 🚊Eminönü)

Understand

Ottoman *Hans*

Built by rich merchants, *hans* (caravanserais) enabled caravans to unload and trade their spices, furs, silks and slaves right in the thick of the bazaar action. Typically two- to three-storey arcaded buildings set around a courtyard where animals could be housed, they differed from Persian-style caravanserais in that they were used as storage and trading spaces as well as for short-term accommodation. Although *hans* are found all over Turkey, the concentration in İstanbul is unrivalled, a testament to the city's importance as a trading-route hub. Sadly, most are in a dilapidated state today.

DAMON LYNCH/SHUTTERSTOCK ©

Domes of the New Mosque (p70)

Siirt Şeref Büryan Kebap

ANATOLIAN €

11 🍴 Map p68, A2

Those who enjoy investigating regional cuisines should head to this four-storey eatery in the Women's Bazaar (p71) near the Aqueduct of Valens. It specialises in two dishes that are a speciality of the southeastern city of Siirt: *büryan* (lamb slow-cooked in a pit) and *perde pilavi* (chicken and rice cooked in pastry). Both are totally delicious. (📞0212-635 8085; http://serefburyan.org; İtfaye Caddesi 4, Kadınlar Pazarı, Fatih; büryan ₺15, perde pilavi ₺15, kebaps ₺13-32; ⏰9.30am-10pm Sep-May, till midnight Jun-Aug; 🅿❄👶; Ⓜ️Vezneciler)

Sur Ocakbaşı

KEBAP €€

12 🍴 Map p68, A2

Indulge in some peerless people watching while enjoying the grilled meats at this popular place in the Women's Bazaar (p71). The square is always full of locals shopping or enjoying a gossip, and tourists were a rare sight before Anthony Bourdain filmed a segment of *No Reservations* here and blew Sur's cover. (📞0212-533 8088; www.surocakbasi.com; İtfaiye Caddesi 27, Fatih; kebaps ₺15-30; ⏰11am-1am; Ⓜ️Vezneciler)

Dürümcü Raif Usta

KEBAP €

13 Map p68, G4

The assembly line of staff assisting the *usta* (grill master) at this place attests to the excellence and popularity of its Adana or Urfa *dürüm kebap* (Adana or Urfa kebap, raw onion and parsley wrapped in lavaş bread). Note that the Adana is spicy; Urfa isn't. (📞0212-528 4910; Küçük Yıldız Han Sokak 6, Mahmutpaşa; dürüm kebap ₺10-12; ⏲11.30am-6pm Mon-Sat; 🚇Çemberlitaş)

Aynen Dürüm

KEBAP €

14 Map p68, G4

This perennially busy place is located just inside the Grand Bazaar's Kılıççılar Gate, near where the currency dealers ply their noisy trade. Patrons are free to doctor their choice of meat (we like the chicken) with pickled cucumber, grilled and pickled green chillies, parsley, sumac and other accompaniments that are laid out on the communal bench. (Muhafazacılar Sokak 29, Grand Bazaar; dürüm kebap ₺9-12; ⏲7am-6pm Mon-Sat; 🚇Çemberlitaş)

Kuru Fasülyeci Erzincanlı Ali Baba

TURKISH €

15 Map p68, D2

Join the crowds of hungry locals at this long-time *fasülyeci* (restaurant specialising in beans) opposite the Süleymaniye Mosque. It's been dishing up its signature *kuru fasülye* (white beans cooked in a spicy tomato sauce) accompanied by pilaf (rice) and *turşu* (pickles) since 1924. The next-door *fasülyeci* is nearly as old and serves up more of the same. No alcohol. (📞0212-514 5878; www.kurufasulyeci.com; Professor Sıddık Sami Onar Caddesi 11, Süleymaniye; beans with pilaf & pickles ₺17; ⏲8am-9pm; 📷; Ⓜ Vezneciler)

Gaziantep Burç Ocakbaşı

KEBAP €

16 Map p68, F4

The *usta* (grill master) at this simple place presides over a charcoal grill where choice cuts of meats are cooked to perfection. You can claim a stool, or ask for a *dürüm* (meat wrapped in bread) kebap to go. We particularly recommend the spicy Adana kebap and the delectable

---

⌕ Local Life

Fish Sandwiches

The city's favourite fast-food treat is undoubtedly the *balık ekmek* (fish sandwich), and the most atmospheric place to try one is at the Eminönü end of the Galata Bridge (Map pXX, H1). Here, in front of fishing boats tied to the quay, are a number of stands where mackerel fillets are grilled, crammed into fresh bread and served with salad; a generous squeeze of bottled lemon is optional but recommended. A sandwich will set you back a mere ₺8 or so, and is delicious accompanied by a glass of the *şalgam* (sour turnip juice, ₺2) sold by nearby pickle vendors.

Spice Bazaar (p70)

dolması (eggplant and red peppers stuffed with rice and herbs). (Parçacılar Sokak 12, off Yağlıkçılar Caddesi, Grand Bazaar; kebaps ₺15-20; ⏱noon-4pm Mon-Sat; 🚇Beyazıt-Kapalı Çarşı)

Dönerci Şahin Usta KEBAP €

18 🍴 Map p68, G4

Turks take family, football and food seriously. And when it comes to food, few dishes are sampled and assessed as widely as the humble döner kebap. Ask any shopkeeper in the Grand Bazaar about who makes the best döner in the immediate area, and he is likely to give the same answer: 'Şahin Usta, of course!'. Takeaway only. (📞0212-526 5297; www.donercisahinusta.com; Kılıççılar Sokak 9, Nuruosmaniye; döner kebap from ₺9; ⏱11am-3pm Mon-Sat; 🚇Çemberlitaş)

Havuzlu Restaurant TURKISH €€

18 🍴 Map p68, F4

After a morning spent in the Grand Bazaar, many visitors choose to park their shopping bags at this well-known *lokanta*. A lovely space with a vaulted ceiling, Havuzlu (named after the small fountain at its entrance) serves up simple but tasty fare to hungry hordes of tourists and shop-keepers – go early when food is fresh-est. No alcohol. (📞0212-527 3346; www.havuzlurestaurant.com; Gani Çelebi Sokak 3, Grand Bazaar; portions ₺17-30; ⏱9am-7pm Mon-Sat; ❄♿; 🚇Beyazıt-Kapalı Çarşı)

Q Local Life
Mimar Sinan Teras Cafe

A magnificent panorama of the city can be enjoyed from the spacious outdoor terrace of this popular student **cafe** (📞0212-514 4414; Mimar Sinan Han, Fetva Yokuşu 34-35, Süleymaniye; ⏰8am-1am; 🛜; Ⓜ Vezneciler) in a ramshackle building located in the shadow of the Süleymaniye Mosque. Come here during the day or in the evening to admire the view over a coffee, unwind with a nargile or enjoy a glass of çay and game of backgammon.

Drinking

Erenler Nargile ve Çay Bahçesi   TEA GARDEN

19 🍷 Map p68, F5

Set in the vine-covered courtyard of the Çorlulu Ali Paşa Medrese, this nargile cafe near the Grand Bazaar is the most atmospheric in the Old City. (Yeniçeriler Caddesi 35, Beyazıt; ⏰7am-midnight; 🚇Beyazıt-Kapalı Çarşı)

Lale Bahçesi   TEA GARDEN

20 🍷 Map p68, D2

Make your way down the stairs into the sunken courtyard opposite the Süleymaniye Mosque to discover this outdoor teahouse, which is popular with students from the nearby theological college and İstanbul University, who head here to enjoy çay and nargiles. (Şifahane Caddesi 2, Süleymaniye; ⏰9am-11pm; Ⓜ Vezneciler)

Ethem Tezçakar Kahveci   CAFE

21 🍷 Map p68, F4

Bekir Tezçakar's family has been at the helm of this tiny coffee shop for four generations. Smack bang in the middle of the bazaar's most glamorous retail strip, its traditional brass-tray tables and wooden stools are a good spot to enjoy a break and watch the passing parade of shoppers. (📞0212-513 2133; Halıcılar Çarşışı Sokak 61-63, Grand Bazaar; ⏰8.30am-6pm Mon-Sat; 🚇Beyazıt-Kapalı Çarşı)

Şark Kahvesi   CAFE

22 🍷 Map pF4

The Şark's arched ceiling betrays its former existence as part of a bazaar street – years ago some enterprising *kahveci* (coffeehouse owner) walled up several sides and turned it into a cafe. Located on one of the bazaar's major thoroughfares, it's popular with both stallholders and tourists, who enjoy tea, coffee (Turkish, espresso and filter) or a cold drink. (Oriental Coffee Shop; 📞0212-512 1144; Yağlıkçılar Caddesi 134, Grand Bazaar; ⏰8.30am-7pm Mon-Sat; 🚇Beyazıt-Kapalı Çarşı)

Vefa Bozacısı   BOZA BAR

23 🍷 Map p68, C2

This famous *boza* bar was established in 1876 and locals still flock here to drink the viscous tonic, which is made from water, sugar and fermented barley and has a slight lemony tang. Topped with dried chickpeas and a sprinkle of cinnamon, it has a reputation for building up strength and virility, and tends to be an acquired taste. (☎0212-519 4922; www.vefa.com.tr; 66 Vefa Caddesi, Molla Hüsrev; boza ₺3; ⊙8am-midnight; Ⓜ Vezneciler)

Shopping

Abdulla Natural Products
TEXTILES, BATHWARE

23 🔒 Map p68, F4

The first of the Western-style designer stores to appear in this ancient marketplace, Abdulla sells top-quality cotton bed linen and towels, hand-spun woollen throws from eastern Turkey, cotton *peştemals* (bath wraps) and pure olive-oil soap. (☎0212-527 3684; www.abdulla.com; Halıcılar Sokak 60, Grand Bazaar; ⊙8.30am-7pm Mon-Sat; 🚇 Beyazıt-Kapalı Çarşı)

Epoque
ANTIQUES

25 🔒 Map pG4

Serious antique shoppers should make their way to this old-fashioned business near the bazaar's Nuruosmaniye Gate. Silver candlesticks and trays, enamelled cigarette cases, jewellery, watches and an extraordinary range of icons are on offer in the elegant shop. The elderly owner and sales members are happy to welcome browsers. (☎0212-527 7865; Sandal Bedesten Sokak 38, Grand Bazaar; ⊙8.30am-7pm Mon-Sat; 🚇 Beyazıt-Kapalı Çarşı)

Altan Şekerleme
FOOD & DRINKS

26 🔒 Map p68, E1

Kids aren't the only ones who like candy stores. İstanbullus of every age have been coming to this shop in the Küçük Pazar (Little Bazaar) precinct below the Süleymaniye Mosque since 1865, lured by its cheap and delectable *lokum* (Turkish Delight), *helva* (sweet made from sesame seeds) and *akide* (hard candy). (☎0212-522 5909; Kıble Çeşme Caddesi 68, Eminönü; ⊙8am-7pm Mon-Sat, 9am-6pm Sun; Ⓜ Haliç)

Derviş
TEXTILES

27 🔒 Map p68, F4

Raw cotton and silk *peştemals* (bath wraps) share shelf space here with traditional Turkish dowry vests and engagement dresses. If these don't take your fancy, the pure olive-oil soaps and old hamam bowls are sure to step into the breach. There's another **branch** (Map p62; Cebeci Han 10, Grand Bazaar; ⊙8.30am-7pm Mon-Sat; 🚇 Beyazıt-Kapalı Çarşı) off Yağlıcılar Caddesi. (☎0212-528 7883; www.dervis.com; Halıcılar Sokak 51, Grand Bazaar; ⊙8.30am-7pm Mon-Sat; 🚇 Beyazıt-Kapalı Çarşı)

Necef Antik & Gold
JEWELLERY

28 🔒 Map p68, F4

Owner Haluk Botasun has been hand-crafting 24-carat gold jewellery in his tiny İç Bedesten store for decades, producing attractive pieces in Byzantine and Ottoman styles. The earrings and cufflinks featuring delicate mosaics are particularly desirable. (📞0212-513 0372; necefantik@outlook.com; Şerifağa Sokak 123, İç Bedesten, Grand Bazaar; ⏰8.30am-7pm Mon-Sat; 🚇Beyazıt-Kapalı Çarşı)

Yazmacı Necdet Danış
TEXTILES

29 🔒 Map p68, F4

Fashion designers and buyers from every corner of the globe know that, when in İstanbul, this is where to come to source top-quality textiles. It's crammed with bolts of fabric of every description – shiny, simple, sheer and sophisticated – as well as *peştemals,* scarves and clothes. Murat Danış next door is part of the same operation. (Yağlıkçılar Caddesi 57, Grand Bazaar; ⏰8.30am-7pm Mon-Sat; 🚇Beyazıt-Kapalı Çarşı)

Dhoku
CARPETS

30 🔒 Map p68, F4

One of the new generation of rug stores opening in the bazaar, Dhoku (meaning 'texture') sells artfully designed wool kilims in resolutely modernist designs. Its sister store, **EthniCon** (Map p62), opposite Dhoku, sells similarly stylish rugs in vivid colours. (📞0212-527 6841; www.dhoku. com; Tekkeçiler Sokak 58-60, Grand Bazaar; ⏰8.30am-7pm Mon-Sat; 🚇Beyazıt-Kapalı Çarşı)

Ümit Berksoy
JEWELLERY

31 🔒 Map p68, G4

Jeweller Ümit Berksoy handcrafts gorgeous Byzantine-style rings, earings and necklaces using gold and old coins at his tiny atelier just outside the İç Bedesten. He also creates contemporary pieces. (📞0212-522 3391; İnciler Sokak 2-6, Grand Bazaar; ⏰8.30am-7pm Mon-Sat; 🚇Vezneciler, 🚇Beyazıt-Kapalı Çarşı)

Mekhann
TEXTILES

32 🔒 Map p68, F5

Bolts of richly coloured, hand-woven silk from Uzbekistan and a range of finely woven shawls join finely embroidered bedspreads and pillow slips on the crowded shelves of this Grand Bazaar store, which sets the bar high when it comes to quality and price. There's another branch near the tram stop in Tophane. (📞0212-519 9444; www.mekhann.com; Divrikli Sokak 49, Grand Bazaar; ⏰8.30am-7pm Mon-Sat; 🚇Beyazıt-Kapalı Çarşı)

Silk & Cashmere
CLOTHING

33 🔒 Map p68, H5

The Nuruosmaniye branch of this popular chain sells cashmere and silk-cashmere-blend cardigans, jumpers, tops and shawls. All are remarkably well priced considering their quality. (📞0212-528 5286; www.silkcashmere.com; Nuruosmaniye Caddesi 38, Nuruosmaniye; ⏰9.30am-7pm Mon-Sat; 🚇Çemberlitaş)

Understand
İstanbul in Print

This colourful and complex city has inspired writers throughout history, and continues to do so today. Local luminaries including Orhan Pamuk and Elif Şafak set most of their novels here, and many foreign writers have used the city as a literary setting.

Local Writers

İrfan Orga's 1950 masterpiece *Portrait of a Turkish Family* is among the best writing about the city ever published, as is *A Mind at Peace* (1949) by Ahmet Hamdi Tanipar. Elif Şafak's *The Flea Palace* (2002), *The Bastard of Istanbul* (2006) and *The Architect's Apprentice* (2014) are more recent novels set in İstanbul.

Nobel laureate Orhan Pamuk has set most of his novels here, including *Cevdet Bey & His Sons* (1982), *The White Castle* (1985), *The Black Book* (1990), *The New Life* (1995), *My Name is Red* (1998), *The Museum of Innocence* (2009) and *A Strangeness in My Mind* (2015). In 2005 he published a memoir, *Istanbul: Memories of a City*.

Literary Visitors

Foreign novelists and travel writers have long tried to capture the magic and mystery of İstanbul in their work. One of the earliest to do so was French novelist Pierre Loti, whose novel *Aziyadé* (1879) introduced Europe to Loti's almond-eyed Turkish lover and to the mysterious and all-pervasive attractions of the city itself. Another notable work from this period is *Constantinople* (1878) by Italian writer Edmondo De Amicis.

Historical novels set here include *The Rage of the Vulture* (Barry Unsworth; 1982), *The Stone Woman* (Tariq Ali; 2001), *The Calligrapher's Night* (Yasmine Ghata; 2006) and *The Dark Angel* (Mika Waltari; 1952).

The city also features as the setting for some great crime novels and thrillers, including Barbara Nadel's Inspector İkmen novels; Joseph Kanon's *Istanbul Passage* (2012); Jason Goodwin's Yashim the Ottoman Investigator novels; Jenny White's Kamil Paşa novels; Mehmet Murat Somer's Hop-Çıkı-Yaya series of gay crime novels; Esmahan Aykol's Kati Hirschel Murder Mysteries; and Eric Ambler's *The Mask of Dimitrios* (1939), *Journey into Fear* (1940) and *The Light of Day* (1962).

Top Sights
Kariye Museum (Chora Church)

Getting There

🚌 **Bus** Lines 28 from Eminönü and 87 from Taksim; Edirnekapı stop.

⛴ **Ferry** Golden Horn (Haliç) line; Ayvansaray stop.

İstanbul has more than its fair share of Byzantine monuments, but few are as drop-dead gorgeous as this mosaic-laden church. Nestled in the shadow of Theodosius II's monumental land walls and now a museum overseen by the curators of Aya Sofya, it receives a fraction of the visitor numbers that its big sister attracts but offers an equally fascinating insight into Byzantine art. Virtually all of the interior decoration – the famous mosaics and the less renowned but equally striking frescoes – dates from 1312.

Inner-narthex mosaic

Inner Narthex

Highlights in the second of the inner corridors include the *Khalke Jesus*, which shows Christ and Mary with two donors. The southern dome features a stunning depiction of Jesus and his ancestors (the *Genealogy of Christ*) and the northern dome features a serenely beautiful mosaic of Mary and the Baby Jesus surrounded by her ancestors.

Nave

In the nave are mosaics of Christ; of Mary and the Baby Jesus; and of the *Assumption of the Blessed Virgin* – turn around to see this, as it's over the main door you just entered. The 'infant' being held by Jesus is actually Mary's soul.

Pareeclesion

This side chapel was built to hold the tombs of the church's founder and relatives. It's decorated with frescoes depicting scenes taken from the Old Testament; most deal with the themes of death and resurrection. The striking painting in the apse shows a powerful Christ raising Adam and Eve out of their sarcophagi, with saints and kings in attendance.

The Chora's Patron

Most of the interior decoration was funded by Theodore Metochites, a poet and man of letters who was auditor of the treasury under Emperor Andronikos II (r 1282–1328). One of the museum's most wonderful mosaics, found above the door to the nave in the inner narthex, depicts Theodore offering the church to Christ.

Kariye Müzesi

☎0212-631 9241

www.choramuseum.com

Kariye Camii Sokak 18, Edirnekapı

adult/child ₺30/free

🕑9am-7pm mid-Apr–late Oct, to 5pm late Oct–mid-Apr, last entry 30min before closing

🚌28 from Eminönü, 87 from Taksim, 🚇Ayvansaray

☑ Top Tips

▶ After visiting the museum, walk downhill to the Vodina Caddesi area near the shore of the Golden Horn for more sights, restaurants and a slice of everyday İstanbul life.

✖ Take a Break

Sample Ottoman dishes fit for a sultan at next-door **Asitane** (☎0212-635 7997; www. asitanerestaurant.com; Kariye Oteli, Kariye Camii Sokak 6, Edirnekapı; starters ₺18-28, mains ₺58 🕑noon-10.30pm).

Explore

İstiklal Caddesi & Beyoğlu

This is the city's high-octane eating, drinking and entertainment hub; full of restaurants, bars and live-music venues. Built around the major boulevard of İstiklal Caddesi it includes a mix of bohemian residential districts such as Çukurcuma, bustling entertainment enclaves, historically rich pockets such as Galata, style hubs including Karaköy and arcades such as the Flower Passage (p83; pictured).

The Sights in a Day

☀ Begin your day at **Taksim Meydanı** (Taksim Square; p84), the symbolic heart of both Beyoğlu and the modern city. From here, wander down **İstiklal Caddesi** (p84), being sure to visit the **Fish Market** (p85) and **ARTER** (p85). Stop for a coffee at **Manda Batmaz** (p99) or a tea along **Hazzo Pulo Pasajı** (p85), then visit Orhan Pamuk's **Museum of Innocence** (p92) in the colourful Çukurcuma district.

☀ Dedicate your afternoon to art. Begin at the **Pera Museum** (p86) and then head downhill to **İstanbul Modern** (p92) to view its diverse collection of Turkish and international art. Afterwards, saunter through neighbouring Karaköy, enjoying a coffee or tea at one of its many hip cafes or a delicious baklava at **Karaköy Güllüoğlu** (p95).

☾ Beyoğlu is known for its rooftop bars, so start your evening at **Mikla** (p97) or **360** (p98). Next, move on to a traditional eatery to eat, drink and make merry à la Turka – **Antiochia** (p94), **Eleos** (p94) and **Zübeyir Ocakbaşı** (p95) are all great options. End the evening at one of the clubs off İstiklal or take in some jazz at **Nardis Jazz Club** (p100).

For a local's day in Beyoğlu, see p88.

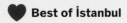

👁 Top Sights
İstiklal Caddesi (p84)

Pera Museum (p86)

🔍 Local Life
Cihangir & Çukurcuma (p88)

♥ Best of İstanbul

Eating

Antiochia (p94)

Zübeyir Ocakbaşı (p95)

Neolokal (p96)

Eleos (p94)

Hayvore (p95)

Karaköy Güllüoğlu (p95)

Karaköy Lokantası (p95)

Meze by Lemon Tree (p96)

Getting There

🚊 **Tram** Alight at Karaköy or Kabataş for funicular connections up to İstiklal Caddesi; it's a steep uphill walk from the Tophane and Fındıklı-MSÜ stops.

Ⓜ **Metro** Take the M2 from Yenikapı or Vezneciler and alight at Haliç for Karaköy; Şişhane for Galata, Tünel, Asmalımescit and the lower half of İstiklal Caddesi; and Taksim for Cihangir, Çukurcuma and the top half of İstiklal Caddesi.

Top Sights

İstiklal Caddesi

Taksim Meydanı

Named after the 18th-century stone *taksim* (water storage unit) on its western side, this square is home to an architecturally significant cultural centre (currently threatened with demolition) and an often-overlooked monument to the founding of the Republic. In recent years, it has also been the site of major anti- and pro-government demonstrations.

Independence Ave

👁 Map p90, C2

Ⓜ Taksim, Şişhane

Street-food vendor on İstiklal Caddesi

Çiçek Pasajı

Built in 1876 and decorated in Second Empire style, the Cité de Pera building once housed a shopping arcade and apartments. The arcade is now known as the **Flower Passage** (Çiçek Pasajı; İstiklal Caddesi; M Taksim) and is full of boisterous *meyhanes* (taverns).

Balık Pazarı

Next to the Çiçek Pasajı, Galatasaray's **Fish Market** (Balık Pazarı; Şahne Sokak, off İstiklal Caddesi, Galatasaray; M Taksim) is full of small stands selling *midye tava* (skewered mussels fried in hot oil), *kokoreç* (skewered lamb or mutton intestines seasoned and grilled over charcoal) and fresh produce.

Hazzo Pulo Pasajı

One of the most interesting aspects of İstiklal is its array of historic shopping *pasajs* (passages) within or between buildings. The most atmospheric of these is this open-air cobbled courtyard near Galatasaray Sq (the intersection of İstiklal with Yeniçarşı Caddesi), which is entered through a narrow passageway lined with tacky jewellery stores. Behind these is a popular *çay bahçesi* (tea garden), secondhand bookshops and an array of old-fashioned boutiques.

ARTER

This four-floor contemporary **arts space** (☎ 0212-708 5800; www.arter.org.tr; İstiklal Caddesi 211; admission free; ⏰ 11am-7pm Tue-Thu, noon-8pm Fri-Sun; M Şişhane, 🚇 Tünel) is housed in a magnificently restored 19th-century building and has an exhibition program featuring big names in the international art world.

☑ **Top Tips**

▶ Start at Taksim Meydanı and walk down İstiklal before heading through historic Galata to Karaköy, next to the Galata Bridge.

▶ The neighbourhoods within Beyoğlu all have distinct and fascinating characters. Be sure to veer off İstiklal during your perambulation to explore districts such as Cihangir, Çukurcuma and Asmalımescit.

✗ **Take a Break**

Hayvore (p95) near the Galatasaray Lycée is one of the city's best *lokantas* (eatery serving ready-made food), serving delicious Black Sea dishes to lunchtime regulars.

During warm weather, the İstiklal branch of popular **Mado** (☎ 0212-245 4631; http://mado.com.tr; İstiklal Caddesi 121; ⏰ 7am-2am; M Taksim), a chain of *dondurma* (Turkish ice cream) cafes, does a roaring trade.

Top Sights
Pera Museum

There's plenty to see at this impressive museum, Pera Müzesi, but the major drawcard is its wonderful exhibition of paintings featuring Turkish Orientalist themes. Drawn from the world-class Kıraç collection, the works provide some insight into the Ottoman world of the 17th to 20th centuries and include the most beloved painting in the Turkish canon – Osman Hamdı Bey's *The Tortoise Trainer* (1906).

👁 Map p90, B3

www.peramuseum.org

Meşrutiyet Caddesi 65, Tepebaşı

adult/student/child under 12yr ₺20/10/free

🕐10am-7pm Tue-Thu & Sat, to 10pm Fri, noon-6pm Sun

Ⓜ Şişhane, 🚇 Tünel

The Tortoise Trainer by Osman Hamdı Bey

Orientalist Paintings

Opulent portraits of sultans, courtiers and ambassadors join quaint scenes of old Stamboul and plenty of depictions of life in the Ottoman harem in this wonderful showcase of Orientalist art.

Osman Hamdı Bey Homage

Art was only one of many strings to Osman Hamdı Bey's bow, but his paintings are probably his best-known and certainly best-loved legacy. Born in 1842, this artist, archaeologist, museum curator and public intellectual had a huge impact on the city's cultural fabric until his death in 1910, and this homage includes famous works such as *Two Musician Girls* (1880) and *The Tortoise Trainer* (1906).

Temporary Exhibition Floors

The museum's upper floors host high-profile temporary exhibitions of international and Turkish art. Big names are regular fixtures, with past exhibitions having showcased the work of Andy Warhol, Giorgio de Chirico, Pablo Picasso, Fernando Botero, Grayson Perry and other luminaries.

Kütahya Tiles and Ceramics

Drawn from the museum's huge collection of Kütahya ceramics and tiles, this regularly refreshed display of pieces manufactured between the 18th and 20th centuries features gorgeously glazed and coloured plates, tiles and coffee sets.

☑ Top Tips

▶ All visitors are given free entry between 6pm and 10pm on Fridays.

▶ Free entry for students on Wednesdays.

▶ The museum has a nearby annexe, the **İstanbul Araştırmaları Enstitüsü** (İstanbul Research Institute; 📞0212-334 0900; http://en.iae.org.tr; Meşrutiyet Caddesi 47, Tepebaşı; admission free; 🕐10am-7pm Mon-Sat; Ⓜ Şişhane, 🚋Tünel), where exhibitions about the cultural and social history of İstanbul are held.

✕ Take a Break

The in-house **Pera Café** (sandwiches ₺15-16, pastas ₺18-20, cakes ₺7-12; 🕐10am-7pm Tue-Thu & Sat, to 10pm Fri, noon-6pm Sun; ❄🛜) on the ground floor is decorated in art-deco style, as befits its location in a building that originally housed the swish Bristol Hotel. It's a comfortable spot for coffee, cake, a glass of wine or a light lunch.

Local Life
Cihangir & Çukurcuma

Cascading down the southern slope from Taksim to the Bosphorus, these two Beyoğlu neighbourhoods have managed to remain both residential and off the usual tourist trail. Spending half a day exploring their steep and winding streets offers a fascinating glimpse into the local's lifestyle.

① People-watching in Firuz Ağa

The cafes surrounding the squat green **Firuz Ağa Mosque** (Taktaki Yakuşu, Cihangir; Ⓜ Taksim) are popular gathering places. Join the locals for a glass of çay under the trees at the Kardeşler Cafe or squeeze into fashionable **Kronotrop** (☏ 0212-249 9271; www.kronotrop.com.tr/en; Firuzağa Cami Sokak 2b, Cihangir; ⏲ 7.30am-9pm Mon-Fri, 10am-10pm Sat, 10am-9pm Sun; 🛜; Ⓜ Taksim) for an expertly made espresso, cold-drip or Turkish coffee.

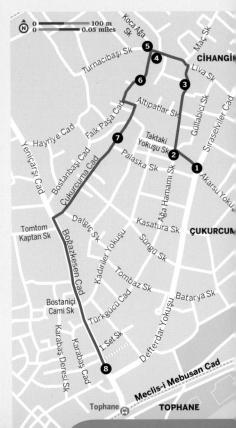

❷ Hot from the Oven

The aged wood-fired oven at tiny bakery-cafe **Datlı Maya** (☏0212-292 9057; www.datlimaya.com; Türkgücü Caddesi 59, Cihangir; breakfast dishes ₺10-35, pides ₺10-22, lahmacuns ₺5-7, cakes & pastries ₺5-10; ⏱9am-10pm Tue-Sun; 🛜🖥; Ⓜ Taksim) produces tasty vegetable *güveçs* (stews), *lahmacuns* (Arabic pizzas) and *pides* (Turkish-style pizza) that local workers and residents order and enjoy while sitting in front of the Firuz Ağa Mosque.

❸ Asri Türşucu

Turks love their pickles, and this long-established **türşucu** (pickle shop; ☏0212-244 4724; Ağa Hamamı Sokak 9a, Çukurcuma; ⏱9am-8.30pm Mon-Sat; Ⓜ Taksim) with its colourful window display is where locals come to buy mouth-puckering vegetables and fruits to use in salads and meze spreads.

❹ Ağa Hamamı

It may not be as attractive – or even as clean – as the tourist hamams in the Old City, but this **bathhouse** (☏0212-249 5027; www.agahamami.com; Turnacıbaşı Caddesi 48, Çukurcuma; ⏱10am-10.30pm; Ⓜ Taksim) is the oldest hamam in the city and a local landmark. Dating from 1454, it was renovated by order of Sultan Abdülmecid I in 1844 and now serves a mixed-sex clientele.

❺ Pizza & Wine

Weekly live jazz sessions, excellent pizzas and an extremely quaffable cheap house wine from Yunatçılar winery on the Aegean island of Bozcaada make **Çukurcuma 49** (☏0212-249 0048; Turnacıbaşı Caddesi 49, Çukurcuma; pizzas ₺18-40; ⏱10.30am-10.30pm; ❄🛜🖥🚻; Ⓜ Taksim) one of the neighbourhood's most popular local hangouts.

❻ Faik Paşa Caddesi

This winding street full of boutiques, antique shops and pretty 19th-century apartment buildings is named after Faik Paşa (1876–1916), a general in the Ottoman army who fought in the Gallipoli campaign.

❼ Foodie Oasis

Enjoying brunch on the front terrace at **Cuma** (☏0212-293 2062; www.cuma. cc; Çukurcuma Caddesi 53a, Çukurcuma; breakfast plate ₺42, lunch dishes ₺19-34, dinner mains ₺30-36; ⏱9am-11pm Mon-Sat, to 8pm Sun; 🛜🖥🚻; Ⓜ Taksim) is high on the weekend 'To Do' list of locals and visitors alike. Fortunately. Banu Tiryakioğulları's seasonally-driven food is also great at other times of the day, when tables on the terrace or in the stylish upstairs dining room are easier to snaffle.

❽ Style Street

In the last couple of years, Boğazkesen Caddesi in Tophane has morphed into one of the city's most interesting retail hubs, dotted with artisan-owned homeware and clothing boutiques. Head down it to browse for stylish souvenirs on your way to the Tophane tram stop.

TÜNEL

Yazgan Sk

Şişhane

Şişhane

Karabaş Cad

Karabaş Deresi Sk

Bostanı Cami Sk

Fevzi Sk

Kumbaracı Yokuşu

Hacı Mimi Külhanı Sk

Galata Mevlevi Museum

Galipdede Cad

Museum of Turkish Jews

Serdar-ı Ekrem Cad

Tatar Beyi Sk

Ali Hoca Sk

Lüleci Hendek Cad

Galata Meydanı

GALATA

Galata Tower

Küçük Hendek Sk

Büyük Hendek Cad

Bankalar Cad

Banker Sk

Kuledibi (Galata Kulesi) Sk

Laleli Çeşme Sk

Okçu Musa Cad

Tersane Cad

Kürekçiler Cad (Lower Station)

Tünel (Lower Station)

Galata

Bilur Sk

SALT Galata

Fish Market (Balık Pazarı)

Galata Bridge (Galata Köprüsü)

Karaköy Meydanı

KARAKÖY

Karaköy Cad

Rıhtım Cad

Gümrük Sk

Arapoğlan Sk

Kemeraltı Cad

Necatibey Cad

Hoca Tahsin Sk

Münihane Cad

Kemankeş Cad

Denizciler

Ali Paşa Medresesi Sk

Ali Paşa Değirmeni Sk

Tophane

Tophane İskele Cad

TOPHANE

İstanbul Modern

Meclis-i Mebusan Cd

(Boğaziçi) Boğazı Sütul Bosphorus

Golden Horn (Haliç)

For reviews see

◉ Top Sights	p84
◉ Sights	p92
⊗ Eating	p94
⊗ Drinking	p97
◉ Entertainment	p99
◉ Shopping	p100

200 m
0.1 miles

Sights

İstiklal Modern
GALLERY

1 ⊙ Map p90, D6

This large, lavishly funded and innovative museum has an extensive collection of Turkish art and also stages a constantly changing and uniformly excellent program of mixed-media exhibitions by high-profile local and international artists. Its permanent home is next to the Bosphorus in Tophane, but the massive Galataport redevelopment project currently under way means that it will temporarily relocate to another site in Beyoğlu some time in 2016/17. (İstanbul Modern Sanat Müzesi; ☑0212-334 7300; www.istanbulmodern.org; Meclis-i Mebusan Caddesi, Tophane; adult/student/child under 12yr ₺25/14/free; ☺10am-6pm Tue, Wed & Fri-Sun, to 8pm Thu; 🚊Tophane)

Museum of Innocence
MUSEUM

2 ⊙ Map p90, C4

The painstaking attention to detail in this fascinating museum/piece of conceptual art will certainly provide every amateur psychologist with a theory or two about its creator, Nobel Prize–winning novelist Orhan Pamuk. Vitrines display a quirky collection of objects that evoke the minutiae of İstanbullu life in the mid- to late 20th century, when Pamuk's novel of the same name is set. (Masumiyet Müzesi; ☑0212-252 9738; www.masumiyetmuzesi. org; Çukurcuma Caddesi, Dalgıç Çıkmazı 2; adult/student ₺25/10; ☺10am-6pm Tue-Sun, to 9pm Thu; 🚊Tophane)

Museum of Turkish Jews
MUSEUM

3 ⊙ Map p90, A6

Housed in a building attached to the Neve Shalom synagogue near the Galata Tower, this museum was established in 2001 to commemorate the 500th anniversary of the arrival of the Sephardic Jews in the Ottoman Empire, and moved to its current location in 2014. The imaginatively curated and chronologically arranged interactive collection comprises photographs, video, sound recordings and objects that document the history of the Jewish people in Turkey. Visitors must have photo ID with them to enter. (500 Yıl Vakfı Türk Musevileri, The Quincentennial Foundation Museum of Turkish Jews; ☑0212-292 6333; www.muze500.com; Büyük Hendek Caddesi 39, Şişhane; adult/child under 12yr ₺20/free; ☺10am-4pm Mon-Thu, to 1pm Fri, to 2pm Sun; Ⓜ️Şişhane, 🚊Tünel)

Galata Mevlevi Museum
MUSEUM

4 ⊙ Map p90, B5

The *semahane* (whirling-dervish hall) at the centre of this *tekke* (dervish lodge) was erected in 1491 and renovated in 1608 and 2009. It's part of a complex including a *meydan-ı şerif* (courtyard), *çeşme* (drinking fountain), *türbesi* (tomb) and *hamuşan* (cemetery). The oldest of six historic

Galata Tower

Mevlevihaneleri (Mevlevi *tekkes*) remaining in İstanbul, the complex was converted into a museum in 1946. (Galata Mevlevihanesi Müzesi; www.galatamevlevihanesimuzesi.gov.tr; Galipdede Caddesi 15, Tünel; admission ₺10; ⊙9am-4pm Tue-Sun; MŞişhane, ⊟Tünel)

Galata Tower TOWER

5 ⊙ Map p90, A6

The cylindrical Galata Tower stands sentry over the approach to 'new' İstanbul. Constructed in 1348 it was the tallest structure in the city for centuries and it still dominates the skyline north of the Golden Horn. Its vertiginous upper balcony offers 360-degree views of the city, but we're not convinced that the view (though spectacular) justifies the steep admission cost. (Galata Kulesi; www.galatakulesi.org; Galata Meydanı, Galata; adult/child under 12yr ₺25/5; ⊙9am-8.30pm; ⊟Karaköy, ⊟Tünel)

SALT Galata CULTURAL CENTRE

6 ⊙ Map p90, A7

The descriptor 'cultural centre' is used a lot in İstanbul, but is often a misnomer. Here at SALT Galata it really does apply. Housed in a magnificent 1892 bank building designed by Alexandre Vallaury and cleverly adapted by local architectural firm Mimarlar Tasarım, the cutting-edge institution offers an exhibition space,

Understand
Jewish İstanbul

The history of Jews in İstanbul is as long as it is fascinating. Jews were granted freedom of religion and worship in Anatolia by the Seljuks (1077–1308), but weren't treated as liberally by the Byzantines in Constantinople. This led many of them to view the Ottomans as saviours, particularly when Mehmet II made the following offer to Jews fleeing Spain in 1492: 'The God has presented me with many lands and ordered me to take care of the dynasty of his servants Abraham and Jacob...Who, amongst you, with the consent of God, would like to settle in İstanbul, live in peace in the shade of the figs and vineyards, trade freely and own property?'

Sadly, this enlightened state didn't last through the centuries, and Jewish Turks were made to feel considerably less welcome when racially motivated 'wealth taxes' were introduced in 1942. Many members of the community emigrated to the newly established nation of Israel between 1947 and 1949 and others left when violence against Jews and other minorities was unleashed in the 1950s.

Approximately 17,000 Jews currently live in Turkey, with 1700 residing in İstanbul. Sephardic Jews make up around 96% of this number, while the rest are primarily Ashkenazic. There are a total of 19 functioning synagogues in the city. For a list of these, and for information about how to visit them, see www.jewish-europe.net/turkey/en/synagogue.

auditorium, arts research library, cafe and glamorous restaurant. (☎0212-334 2200; www.saltonline.org/en; Bankalar Caddesi 11, Karaköy; admission free; ⊙noon-8pm Tue-Sat, to 6pm Sun; 🚊Karaköy)

Eating

Antiochia   SOUTHEASTERN ANATOLIA €€

7 🍴 Map p90, A5

Dishes from the southeastern city of Antakya (Hatay) are the speciality here. Cold mezes feature olives and wild herbs, and hot choices include delicious *içli köfte* (ground lamb and onion with a bulgar coating)and *özel peyniri* (special fried cheese). Kebaps are exceptional – try the succulent *şiş et* (grilled lamb). Set-menu dinners offer excellent value and there's a 20% discount at lunch, when pides reign supreme. (☎0212-244 0820; www.antiochiaconcept.com; General Yazgan Sokak 3, Tünel; mezes & salads ₺13-18, pides ₺21-22, kebaps ₺24-52; ⊙noon-midnight Mon-Sat; ❄🛜🚻; 🚊Tünel)

Eleos   MEYHANE €€€

8 🍴 Map p90, B5

Hidden upstairs in the shabby Hıdivyal Palas building, Eleos transports its diners from Beyoğlu to the Greek islands. A stylish blue-and-white decor and fabulous Bosphorus view set the scene, and the food seals the deal – colourful mezes featuring plenty of herbs and garlic, tender octopus and calamari, perfectly grilled fish, and fresh fruit to finish. Advance bookings essential. (📞0212-244 9090; www.eleosrestaurant.com; 2nd fl, İstiklal Caddesi 231, Tünel; mezes ₺10-30, mains from ₺30; ⏰2.30pm-midnight; ❄🛜♿; Ⓜ️Şişhane, 🚇Tünel)

Hayvore   LOKANTA ₺

9 ✖️ Map p90, C2

Notable *lokantas* (traditional eateries serving ready-made dishes) are few and far between in modern-day Beyoğlu, so the existence of this bustling place next to the Galatasaray Lycée is to be wholeheartedly celebrated. Specialising in Black Sea cuisine, its delicious leafy greens, pilafs, *hamsi* (fresh anchovy) dishes, soups and pides (Turkish-style pizza) are best enjoyed at lunch so early to score a table. (📞0212-245 7501; www.hayvore.com; Turnacıbaşı Sokak 4, Galatasaray; soups ₺6-10, pides ₺16-23, portions ₺10-20; ⏰11.30am-11pm; ❄🛜♿; Ⓜ️Taksim)

Karaköy Lokantası   TURKISH ₺₺

10 ✖️ Map p90, C7

Known for its gorgeous tiled interior, genial owner and bustling vibe, Karaköy Lokantası serves tasty and well-priced food to its loyal local clientele. It functions as a *lokanta*

(eatery serving ready-made food) during the day, but at night it morphs into a *meyhane* (tavern), with slightly higher prices. Bookings are essential for dinner. (📞0212-292 4455; www.karakoylokantasi.com; Kemankeş Caddesi 37a, Karaköy; mezes ₺10-24, lunch portions ₺13-25, mains ₺28-55; ⏰noon-4pm & 6pm-midnight Mon-Sat, 6pm-midnight Sun; ❄🛜; 🚇Karaköy)

Zübeyir Ocakbaşı   KEBAP ₺₺

11 ✖️ Map p90, D1

Every morning the chefs at this popular *ocakbaşı* (grill house) prepare fresh, top-quality meat – spicy chicken wings and Adana kebaps, flavoursome ribs, pungent liver kebaps and well-marinated lamb *şiş* kebaps – to be grilled over handsome copper-hooded barbecues that night. The offerings are famous throughout the city, so booking a table is essential. (📞0212-293 3951; Bekar Sokak 28; mezes ₺10, kebaps ₺28-38; ⏰noon-midnight; ❄🛜; Ⓜ️Taksim)

Karaköy Güllüoğlu   SWEETS, BÖREK ₺

12 ✖️ Map p90, B7

This much-loved *baklavacı* (baklava shop) opened in 1949 and was the first İstanbul branch of a business established in Gaziantep in the 1820s. A family feud has since led to the opening of other Güllüoğlu offshoots around town, but this remains the best. Pay for a *porsiyon* (portion) of whatever takes your fancy at the register, then order at the counter.

(☎0212-293 0910; www.karakoygulluoglu.
com; Katlı Otopark, Kemankeş Caddesi,
Karaköy; portion baklava ₺8-17, portion börek
₺7.50-8; ⏱7am-11pm Sun-Thu, 8am-11.30pm
Fri & Sat; 🛗; 🚇Karaköy)

Neolokal

MODERN TURKISH €€€

13 ✗ Map p90, A7

Chef Maksut Aşkar opened this
swish eatery in late 2014 and has
been wowing local and international
diners with his exciting twists on
traditional Turkish food ever since.
Utilising ingredients listed on the
Slow Food Foundation's Ark of Taste,
his refined and delicious dishes are
enjoyed alongside the spectacular
Old City views offered by both the
dining room and terrace. (☎0212-244
0016; www.neolokal.com; 1st fl, SALT Galata,
Bankalar Caddesi 11, Karaköy; mains ₺42-62;
⏱6-11pm Tue-Sun; ❄🛜; 🚇Karaköy)

Top Tip

Eating in İstanbul

İstanbul Eats (p142) is a popular
blog investigating the traditional
food culture of the city and is a
great resource for those interested
in seeking out local eateries and
food districts. The team who put it
together also conducts excellent
culinary walks.

Meze by Lemon Tree

MODERN TURKISH €€€

14 ✗ Map p90, A4

Chef Gençay Üçok creates some of
the most interesting and delicious
modern Turkish food seen in the city
and serves it in an intimate restaurant
opposite the Pera Palace Hotel. Regulars tend to opt for the degustation
menu, or choose from the wonderful
array of hot and cold mezes, rather
than ordering mains. Bookings essential. (☎0212-252 8302; www.mezze.com.
tr; Meşrutiyet Caddesi 83b, Tepebaşı; mezes
₺14-39, mains ₺40-56, 4-course degustation
menu for 2 ₺196; ⏱6pm-midnight; ❄🖉;
Ⓜ Şişhane, 🚇Tünel)

Helvetia Lokanta

TURKISH €

15 ✗ Map p90, A5

This tiny *lokanta* with its open kitch-
en is popular with locals, who head
here to enjoy the freshly prepared,
vegetarian-friendly fare. Choose up to
five of the home-style dishes for your
plate and enjoy them in the relaxed
dining space. No alcohol, and cash
only. (☎0212-245 8780; General Yazgan
Sokak 8a, Tünel; mixed plate ₺12.50-15;
⏱noon-10pm Mon-Sat; 🖉; Ⓜ Şişhane,
🚇Tünel)

İnci Pastanesi

DESSERTS €

16 ✗ Map p90, D1

A Beyoğlu institution, İnci was forced
out of its historic İstiklal Caddesi
premises in 2012, but has reopened
here and continues to delight devotees

Streetside cafe, Beyoğlu

with its profiteroles covered in chocolate sauce. We're also particularly partial to the moist chocolate cake filled with candied fruit, but usually ask the staff to hold the chocolate topping. (Mis Sokak 18; profiteroles ₺7; ⏱7am-midnight; ❄; Ⓜ Taksim)

Drinking

Mikla
BAR

17 📍 Map p90, A4

It's worth overlooking the occasional bit of uppity service at this stylish rooftop bar to enjoy excellent cocktails and what could well be the best view in İstanbul. In winter the drinking action moves to the bar in the

upmarket restaurant one floor down. (📞0212-293 5656; www.miklarestaurant. com; Marmara Pera Hotel, Meşrutiyet Caddesi 15, Tepebaşı; ⏱from 6pm Mon-Sat summer only; Ⓜ Şişhane, 🚋 Tünel)

Federal Coffee Company
CAFE

18 📍 Map p90, A6

Our favourite of the recent tsunami of coffee roasteries to open in the city, the Federal Coffee Company advertises itself as an 'Australian Coffee Roaster' and visitors from Down Under will certainly feel at home when sipping a perfectly executed espresso-style coffee in its stylish surrounds. Couches, reading materials and wi-fi make it a perfect caffeine-fuelled workspace. (☎0212-245 0903; www.federal.coffee; Küçük Hendek Caddesi 7, Galata; ◷8am-midnight; ☎; Ⓜ Şişhane, 🚊Tünel)

Unter   BAR

19 🍷 Map p90, C6

This scenester-free zone epitomises the new Karaköy style: it's glam without trying too hard, and has a vaguely arty vibe. Ground-floor windows open to the street in fine weather, allowing the action to spill outside during busy periods. (☎0212-244-5151; www.unter.com.tr; Kara Ali Kaptan Sokak 4, Karaköy; ◷9am-midnight Tue-Thu & Sun, to 2am Fri & Sat; ☎; 🚊Tophane)

360   BAR

20 🍷 Map p90, B3

İstanbul's most famous bar, and deservedly so. If you can score one of the bar stools on the terrace you'll be happy indeed – the view is truly extraordinary. It morphs into a club after midnight on Friday and Saturday, when a cover charge of ₺50 applies

Q Local Life

Manda Batmaz

İstanbullus love to sip Cemil Pilik's viscous yet smooth Turkish coffee, and many make a beeline to this tiny **coffeeshop** (Olivia Geçidi 1a, off İstiklal Caddesi; ◷10am-11pm; Ⓜ Şişhane, 🚊Tünel) whenever they find themselves on İstiklal Caddesi.

(this includes one drink). The food is overpriced and underwhelming – don't bother with dinner. (☎0533 691 0360; www.360istanbul.com; 8th fl, İstiklal Caddesi 163; ◷noon-2am Sun-Thu, to 4am Fri & Sat; ☎; Ⓜ Şişhane, 🚊Tünel)

Alex's Place   BAR

21 🍷 Map p90, B4

A hole-in-the-wall speakeasy in the heart of the Asmalımescit entertainment precinct, this place is beloved of local bohemians who work in the arts and cultural sectors. American owner Alex Waldman is passionate about cocktails and his craft creations have been known to convert beer and wine drinkers alike. (Gönül Sokak 7, Asmalımescit; ◷6pm-1am Tue-Sat; Ⓜ Şişhane, 🚊Tünel)

CUE İstiklal   CLUB

22 🍷 Map p90, C3

A magnificent view, large dance floor, decent sound system and well-made cocktails are the draws at this popular temple to electronica. Check its Twitter and Facebook feeds for who is playing/spinning the deep house, techno and tech house soundtrack. (☎0536 460 7137; 5th fl, Yeniçarşı Caddesi 38, Galatasaray; cover varies; ◷10pm-4am Tue-Sat; Ⓜ Şişhane, 🚊Tünel)

Geyik   BAR, CAFE

23 🍷 Map p90, D4

A hybrid coffee roastery and cocktail bar? Yep, you read that correctly. Run by one-time Turkish barista champion Serkan İpekli and mixologist Yağmur Engin, this ultra-fashionable place is popular with coffee aficionados during the day and barflies at night. On Friday and Saturday evenings it's so crowded that the action spills out of the wood-panelled interior onto the street. (📞0532 773 0013; Akarsu Yokuşu 22, Cihangir; ⏰10am-2am; Ⓜ Taksim)

Indigo   CLUB

26 🚇 Map p90, B3

Its popularity has waxed and waned over the years, but Beyoğlu's four-floor electronic music temple is back in big-time favour with the city's dance-music enthusiasts. The program spotlights top-notch local and visiting DJs or live acts, focusing on house, tech house and tech disco, with an occasional electro-rock number thrown into the mix. Smokers congregate on the upstairs terrace. (📞0212-244 8567; http://indigo-istanbul.com; 1st-5th fl, 309 Akarsu Sokak, Galatasaray; cover varies; ⏰11.30pm-5am Fri & Sat, closed summer; Ⓜ Şişhane, 🚆Tünel)

Karabatak   CAFE

25 🚇 Map p90, C6

Importing dark-roasted Julius Meinl coffee from Vienna, Karabatak's baristas use it to conjure up some of Karaköy's best brews. The outside seating is hotly contested, but the quiet tables inside can be just as alluring. Choose from filter, espresso or Turkish coffee and order a panino or

sandwich if you're hungry. (📞0212-243 6993; www.karabatak.com; Kara Ali Kaptan Sokak 7, Karaköy; ⏰8.30am-10pm Mon-Fri, 9.30am-10pm Sat & Sun; 🛜; 🚆Tophane)

Solera   WINE BAR

26 🚇 Map p90, C3

Stocking more than 300 Turkish wines and pouring an extraordinary 100 by the glass, this atmospherically lit cavern is the city's best wine bar. Regulars tend to head here after work for a glass accompanied by a cheese plate (₺22); many stay on for a perfectly cooked steak (₺35). Bookings are essential on Friday and Saturday night. (📞0212-252 2719; Yeniçarşı Caddesi 44, Galatasaray; ⏰11am-2am; 🛜; Ⓜ Şişhane, 🚆Tünel)

Old Java   CAFE

27 🚇 Map p90, B6

It's all about the beans. Here they roast their own, make a good brew and offer it in hip surrounds where 'bean raves', hipster beards, tats and DJs are par for the course. (📞0212-243 9455; Tartar Beyi Sokak 8, Galata; ⏰10.30am-8pm; 🛜; Ⓜ Şişhane, 🚆Tünel)

Entertainment

Galata Mevlevi Museum   PERFORMING ARTS

28 ⭐ Map p90, B5

The 15th-century *semahane* (whirling-dervish hall) at this *tekke* (dervish lodge) is the venue for a one-hour *sema* (ceremony) held on Sundays throughout the year. Come early to buy your ticket. (Galata Mevlevihanesi Müzesi; www.galatamevlevihanesimuzesi.gov.tr; Galipdede Caddesi 15, Tünel; ₺70; ⊙performances 5pm Sun; MŞişhane, 🚋Tünel)

Nardis Jazz Club   JAZZ

29 ⭐ Map p90, A6

Named after a Miles Davis track, this intimate venue near the Galata Tower is run by jazz guitarist Önder Focan and his wife Zuhal. Performers include gifted amateurs, local jazz luminaries and visiting international artists. It's small, so you'll need to book if you want a decent table. There's a limited dinner/snack menu. (📞0212-244 6327; www.nardisjazz.com; Kuledibi Sokak 14, Galata; cover varies; ⊙9.30pm-12.30am Mon-Thu, 10.30pm-1.30am Fri & Sat, closed Jul & Aug; MŞişhane, 🚋Tünel)

Salon   LIVE MUSIC

30 ⭐ Map p90, A5

This intimate performance space in the İstanbul Foundation for Culture & Arts (İKSV) building hosts live contemporary music (classical, jazz, rock, alternative and world music) as well as theatrical and dance performances. Check its Facebook and Twitter feeds for program details and book through Biletix (p16) or the venue's box office. (📞0212-334 0700; www.saloniksv.com; ground fl, İstanbul Foundation for Culture & Arts, Sadi Konuralp Caddesi 5, Şişhane; ⊙Oct-May; MŞişhane, 🚋Tünel)

Garajistanbul   CULTURAL CENTRE

31 ⭐ Map p90, B3

This performance space occupies a former parking garage in a narrow street behind İstiklal Caddesi and is about as edgy as the city's performance scene gets. It hosts contemporary dance performances, poetry readings, theatrical performances and live music (especially jazz). (📞0212-244 4499; www.garajistanbul.org; Kaymakem Reşat Bey Sokak 11a, Galatasaray; MŞişhane, 🚋Tünel)

Borusan Art   PERFORMING ARTS

32 ⭐ Map p90, B4

An exciting privately funded cultural centre on İstiklal, Borusan is housed in a handsome building and hosts classical, jazz, world and new music concerts in its music hall. The occasional dance performance is included in its schedule. (Borusan Sanat; 📞0212-705 8700; www.borusansanat.com/en; İstiklal Caddesi 160a; MŞişhane, 🚋Tünel)

Shopping

Nahıl   HANDICRAFTS, BATHWARE

33 🔒 Map p90, D1

The felting, lacework, embroidery, all-natural soaps and soft toys in this lovely shop are made by economically

OGUZ DIRBAKAN/SHUTTERSTOCK ©

Cemetery, Galata Mevlevi Museum (p92)

disadvantaged women in Turkey's rural areas. All profits are returned to them, ensuring that they and their families have better lives. (📞0212-251 9085; www.nahil.com.tr; Bekar Sokak 17, Taksim; ⏰10am-7pm Mon-Sat; Ⓜ Taksim)

Hiç   HOMEWARES, HANDICRAFTS

34 🔒 Map p90, B6

Interior designer Emel Güntaş is one of İstanbul's style icons and this recently opened contemporary crafts shop in Tophane is a favourite destination for the city's design mavens. The stock includes cushions, carpets, kilims (pileless woven rugs), silk scarves, lamps, furniture, glassware,

porcelain and felt crafts. Everything here is artisan-made and absolutely gorgeous. (📞0212-251 9973; www.hiccrafts. com; Lüleci Hendek Caddesi 35, Tophane; ⏰10.30am-7pm Mon-Sat; 🚋 Tophane)

NYKS   HOMEWARES

35 🔒 Map p90, B5

Olive-oil candles scented with mint, thyme, bay leaf, pine, lavender, cedar, bergamot, rosemary and green mandarin are presented in gorgeous copper, marble, glass and ceramic containers and offered at this cute shop on one of the city's most attractive shopping streets. Well priced and unusual, they are excellent souvenirs to take home or give to friends and family. (☏0212-252 6957; www.nyks. com.tr; Serdar-ı Ekrem Sokak 49/1a, Galata; Ⓜ Şişhane, 🚋 Tünel)

Artrium   ART, JEWELLERY

36 🔒 Map p90, A5

Crammed with antique ceramics, calligraphy, maps, prints and jewellery, this Aladdin's cave of a shop is most notable for its exquisite miniatures. (☏0212-251 4302; www.artrium.com.tr; Müellif Sokak 12, Tünel; ⓧ9am-7pm Mon-Sat; Ⓜ Şişhane, 🚋 Tünel)

Denizler Kitabevi   MAPS

37 🔒 Map p90, B4

One of the few interesting shops remaining on İstiklal, Denizler Kitabevi sells antique maps, books, prints, photographs and postcards. (☏0212-249 8893; www.denizlerkitabevi.com; İstiklal Caddesi 199a; ⓧ10am-8pm Mon-Sat, noon-8pm Sun; Ⓜ Şişhane, 🚋 Tünel)

Eyüp Sabri Tuncer   BEAUTY

38 🔒 Map p90, C7

Turks of every age adore the colognes and beauty products produced by this local company, which was established in 1923. Its *doğal zeytınyağlı* (natural olive oil) body balms and soaps are wonderfully inexpensive considering their quality. (☏0212-244 0098; www. eyupsabrituncer.com; Mumhane Caddesi 10, Karaköy; ⓧ10am-7pm; 🚋 Karaköy)

Hamm   HOMEWARES

39 🔒 Map p90, C4

Its location on Boğazkesen Caddesi, near the Tophane tram stop, is one of Beyoğlu's style hubs, and Hamm is a great place to garner an understanding of contemporary Turkish style. It showcases furniture, lighting and homewares designed and made in İstanbul. (☏0533 234 1122; www.hamm. com.tr; Boğazkesen Caddesi 71a, Tophane; ⓧ10am-7pm Mon-Sat, 11am-5pm Sun; 🚋 Tophane)

Mabel Çikolata   FOOD

40 🔒 Map p90, B7

The city's most beloved chocolate company started trading in 1947 and neither its logo nor this flagship store have changed much since that time. The milk, dark and flavoured varieties are equally delicious, and retro treats such as the chocolate umbrellas are perennially popular. There's another branch in Nişantaşı. (☏0212-244 3462; www.mabel.com.tr; Gümrük Sokak 11, Karaköy; ⓧ9am-7pm Mon-Fri, to 4pm Sat; 🚋 Karaköy)

Misela   FASHION & ACCESSORIES

41 🔒 Map p90, A4

No self-respecting local fashionista would be without a chic handbag designed by local gal Serra Türker. Quality materials and skill are the hallmarks, for which you will pay accordingly. (☏0212-243 5300; www.

Rugs on display

miselaistanbul.com; Meşrutiyet Caddesi 107e, Tepebaşı; ⊙11am-7pm Mon-Thu, to 8pm Fri, noon-8pm Sat; Ⓜ Şişhane, 🚊 Tünel)

Opus3a

MUSIC

42 🔒 Map p90, E4

Those keen to supplement their CD or vinyl collections with some Turkish music should head to this large shop in Cihangir, where knowledge-able English-speaking staff can steer you towards the best local classical, jazz, alternative and pop recordings. (📞0212-251 8405; www.opus3a.com; Cihangir Caddesi 3a, Cihangir; ⊙11am-8.30pm, to 9.30pm Jun-Aug; Ⓜ Taksim)

Explore

Dolmabahçe Palace & Ortaköy

The stretch of Bosphorus shore between Beşiktaş and Ortaköy is home to the splendid Ottoman-era buildings of Dolmabahçe, Yıldız and Çırağan. North of this picturesque palace precinct is the famous 'Golden Mile', a string of upmarket nightclubs running between the waterside suburbs of Ortaköy and Kuruçeşme, once humble fishing villages and now prime pockets of real estate.

The Sights in a Day

☀ Beat the queues by arriving at **Dolmabahçe Palace** (p106; pictured) as soon as it opens. After taking the compulsory guided tour and visiting the **National Palaces Painting Museum** (p107), enjoy a tea and *tost* (toasted sandwich) at the waterside **Saat Kule Cafe** (p113).

☀ Those who haven't yet reached Ottoman overload could then head to the **Palace Collections Museum** (p111) housed in the former Dolmabahçe Palace kitchens. Alternatively, the impressive new wing of the **İstanbul Naval Museum** (p111) showcases a spectacular collection of imperial *caïques* (decorated rowboats). Afterwards, consider having a drink on the terrace of the ritzy **Çırağan Palace Kempinski Hotel** (p113).

☾ After dinner at **Vogue** (p112) or **Banyan** (p112), kick on to party with the glitterati against the illuminated backdrop of the monumental Bosphorus Bridge at **Reina** (p113) or **Sortie** (p113).

For a local's day in Ortaköy, see p108.

◉ Top Sights

Dolmabahçe Palace (p106)

◯ Local Life

Weekend Wander in Ortaköy (p108)

♥ Best of İstanbul

Architecture

Dolmabahçe Palace (p106)

Çırağan Palace (p112)

Museums

National Palaces Painting Museum (p107)

İstanbul Naval Museum (p111)

Nightlife

Reina (p113)

Sortie (p113)

Getting There

🚌 **Bus** Lines 22 and 25E from Kabataş; 40, 40T and 42T travel from Taksim.

⛴ **Ferry** A few commuter ferries travel from Eminönü to Beşiktaş (daily) and continue on to Ortaköy (Monday to Saturday) in the early evening; there are no return services.

Ⓜ **Metro** A new metro line linking Kabataş and Mahmutbey is scheduled to open in 2017 and will include a stop in Beşiktaş.

Top Sights
Dolmabahçe Palace

These days it's fashionable for architects and critics influenced by the less-is-more aesthetic of the Bauhaus masters to sneer at buildings such as Dolmabahçe. However, the crowds that throng to this imperial pleasure palace with its magnificent Bosphorus location, formal garden, neoclassic exterior and over-the-top interior clearly don't share that disdain, flocking here to visit its Selâmlık (Ceremonial Suites), Harem and Veliaht Dairesi (Apartments of the Crown Prince).

Dolmabahçe Sarayı

👁 Map p110, A4

www.millisaraylar.gov.tr

Dolmabahçe Caddesi, Beşiktaş

adult Selâmlık ₺30, Harem ₺20, joint ticket ₺40

🕑 9am-4pm Tue, Wed & Fri-Sun

🚇 Kabataş

Mustafa Kemal Atatürk's bedroom

Selâmlık

The palace's state apartments were decorated by Frenchman Charles Séchan, designer of the Paris Opera, and are highly theatrical in appearance. They feature a crystal staircase manufactured by Baccarat, mirrored fireplaces, parquet floors, and Sèvres and Yıldız (locally made) porcelain. The most impressive room is the huge Muayede Salon (Ceremonial Hall), which features a purpose-woven 124-sq-metre Hereke carpet and a crystal chandelier weighing 4.5 tonnes.

Harem

Decoration of the Harem is relatively restrained by Dolmabahçe standards (which, of course, isn't saying much). Its most notable elements are the hand-painted ceilings, which feature throughout. The tour passes bedrooms, private salons, a circumcision room and a nursery.

Atatürk's Deathbed

Dolmabahçe was used by the first president of the Republic when he visited İstanbul, and he died here on 10 November 1938. The Harem tour pauses at his bedroom, which features a bed draped in the Turkish flag and a clock stopped at 9.05am, when the great man drew his last breath.

National Palaces Painting Museum

Reopened in 2014 after a long restoration, the Veliaht Dairesi now house the **National Palaces Painting Museum** (Milli Saraylar Resim Müzesi; ☎0212-236 9000; www.millisaraylar.gov.tr; Dolmabahçe Caddesi, Beşiktaş; admission ₺20; ⏱9am-4pm Tue, Wed & Fri-Sun; 🚊Akaretler, 🚊Kabataş), which showcases the palace's collection of paintings. Highlights include the downstairs 'Turkish Painters 1870–1890' room, which includes two Osman Hamdi Bey works, and the upstairs 'İstanbul views' room, which is home to 19th-century street scenes by Germain Fabius Brest.

☑ Top Tips

▶ Visitor numbers in the palace are limited to 3000 per day and this ceiling is often reached on weekends and holidays – come midweek if possible, and even then be prepared to queue (often for a long period and in full sun).

▶ If you arrive before 3pm in summer or 2pm in winter, you must buy a combined ticket to tour both the Selâmlık and Harem; after those times you can take only one tour (we recommend opting for the Selâmlık).

▶ Entry to the National Palaces Painting Museum housed in the Apartments of the Crown Prince behind the Harem and to the Palace Collections Museum in the former kitchens is included in the combined ticket.

✕ Take a Break

The on-site Saat Kule Cafe (p113) has premium Bosphorus views and reasonable prices.

Q Local Life
Weekend Wander in Ortaköy

The settlement of Ortaköy (Turkish for 'Middle Village') dates back to Byzantine times, when it was a small fishing village. These days the picturesque cobbled laneways surrounding its waterside square, known as İskele (Ferry Dock) Meydanı, are filled with cafes, bars and fast-food stands. On Sundays a handicrafts market draws visitors from across the city.

1 İskele Meydanı

Locals love to promenade around this attractive square, which fronts the water and has a backdrop of old timber houses now functioning as restaurants and cafes. In its centre is a pretty 18th-century *çeşme* (fountain). On Sundays the streets surrounding the square are crammed with market stalls.

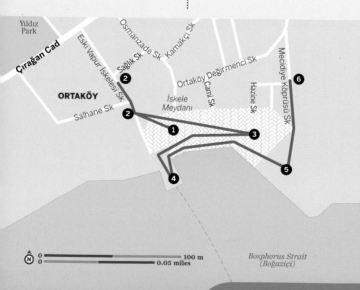

➋ Waterside Brunch

İstanbullus love to brunch, especially if they can do so in glamorous surrounds. Both **The House Cafe** (📞0212-227 2209; www.thehousecafe.com; İskele Meydanı 42; breakfast platter for 1/2 ₺33/52, tost ₺19.50-25, pizzas ₺24-39, mains ₺35; ⊘8am-1am; 🛜; 🚊Kabataş Lisesi) and **Kitchenette** (📞0212-236 9648; www.kitchenette.com.tr; cnr Eski Vapur İslelesi & Sağlık Sokaks, Ortaköy; mains ₺40; ⊘8am-midnight; 🛜; 🚊Kabataş Lisesi) have million-lira waterside locations and are perennially packed on weekends.

➌ Sampling Dondurma

Originating in the southeastern region of Maraş, *dondurma* (Turkish ice cream) is made with salep (ground dried orchid root) and mastic (pine-flavoured resin from the mastic tree) as well as milk and sugar. These unusual ingredients give the ice cream a distinctive chewy texture. To sample some, join the queue at local favourite, **Mado** (📞0212-227 3876; http://mado.com. tr; İskele Meydanı, Ortaköy; ice cream & baklava each from ₺10; ⊘7am-2am; 🚊Ortaköy).

➍ Bosphorus Cruise

Most tourists take a crowded excursion ferry at Eminönü to cruise the Bosphorus, but many locals opt to hop aboard the Short Bosphorus Tour with İstanbul Şehir Hatları (p148), which departs from Eminönü and takes passengers aboard at the Ortaköy İskelesı (Ortaköy Ferry Dock) at 3pm daily for a 1½-hour cruise up to İstinye and back.

➎ Photo Shoot

With the modern Bosphorus (aka Martyrs of July 15) Bridge looming behind it, the 19th-century baroque-style **Ortaköy Mosque** (Ortaköy Camii, Büyük Mecidiye Camii; İskele Meydanı, Ortaköy; 🚊Ortaköy) provides a fabulous photo opportunity for those wanting to illustrate İstanbul's 'old meets new' character. Designed by Nikoğos Balyan, one of the architects of Dolmabahçe Palace, the elegant mosque was built for Sultan Abdül Mecit I between 1853 and 1855, and recently underwent a meticulous restoration. In the light and airy interior, look for several masterful examples of Arabic calligraphy executed by Abdül Mecit, who was an accomplished calligrapher.

➏ Kümpir & Waffle Stands

The pedestrianised street behind the mosque is crowded with stands selling *kümpir* (stuffed baked potatoes) and sweet-smelling waffles. Either makes a perfect mid-afternoon snack.

KURUÇEŞME

Muallim Naci Cad

11
10

Bosphorus (Martyrs of July 15) Bridge

MECİDİYE

İskele Meydanı

6

Ortaköy Dereboyu Cad

Gültekin Sk

Museyi

Mesarlığı Lozan Sk

Sabibal Sk

Fıstıklı Köşk Sk

Çevirmeci Sk

ORTAKÖY

Bosphorus Strait (Boğaziçi)

For reviews see
Top Sights   p106
Sights   p111
Eating   p112
Drinking   p113

500 m
0.25 miles

N

9 Palanga Cad

3 Yıldız Park

YILDIZ

Yahya Efendi Sk

Çırağan Cad

4 8
Çırağan Palace

Yıldız Şale

Müvezzi Cad

Aşariye Sk

EskiKonak Sk

Çiftenbik Sk

Serencebey Yokuşu

Beşiktaş Yalı Sk

Yıldız Cad

İhlamur

Barbaros Bul

Yıldız Cad

Eski Yıldız Cad

İstanbul Naval Museum

İskele Cad

1

2 Beşiktaş Museum

İhlamur Yıldız Cad

Çömezler Sk

Abbasağa Park

Selamlık Sk

Köyiçi Sk

BEŞİKTAŞ

Dolmabahçe Collections Museum

Yıldız Posta Cad

NİŞANTAŞI

DİKİLİTAŞ

Barış Sk

Fulya Deresi Sk

Uzuncaova Cad

Odalar Sk

Dizi Sk

Mısırlı Bahç Sk

Nüzhetiye Cad

Hattat Tahsin Sk

5

2

Süleyman Seba (Spor) Cad

3

Dolmabahçe Cad

7 Dolmabahçe Palace

4

PAVEL DUDEK/SHUTTERSTOCK ©

Ship decoration, İstanbul Naval Museum

Sights

İstanbul Naval Museum   MUSEUM

1 ◉ Map p110, B3

Established over a century ago to celebrate and commemorate Turkish naval history, this museum has been undergoing a prolonged and major renovation. Its architecturally noteworthy copper-clad exhibition hall opened in 2013 and showcases a spectacular collection of 19th-century imperial caïques, ornately decorated wooden rowboats used by the royal household. Temporary exhibitions take place in the downstairs gallery. (İstanbul Deniz Müzesi; ☎ 0212-327 4345; www.denizmuzeleri.tsk.tr; Beşiktaş Caddesi 6, Beşiktaş; adult/student & child ₺6.50/free; ⊙ 9am-5pm Mon-Fri, 10am-6pm Sat & Sun mid-May–mid-Oct, 9am-5pm Tue-Sun mid-Oct–mid-May; 🚌 Bahçeşehir Ünv.)

Palace Collections Museum   MUSEUM

2 ◉ Map p110, A3

Occupying the warehouselike Dolmabahçe Palace kitchens, this museum exhibits items used in the royal palaces and pavilions during the late Ottoman Empire and early Turkish Republic. It is a fascinating hotchpotch of some 5000 objects, including palace portraits and photos, teasets, tiled Islamic wall inscriptions, prayer rugs and embroidery. Hereke carpets and Yıldız Porselen Fabrikası porcelain are also here. (Saray Koleksiyonları Müzesi; ☎0212-236 9000; www.millisaraylar. gov.tr; Beşiktaş Caddesi, Beşiktaş; adult/child ₺5/2; ☺9am-5pm Tue-Sun; 🚌Akaretler, 🚌Kabataş)

Yıldız Park PARK

3 ◉ Map p110, C2

This large and leafy retreat is alive with birds, picnicking families and young couples strolling hand in hand. The best time to visit is in April, when the spring flowers (including thousands of tulips) are in bloom. At the park's highest point is **Yıldız Şale** (Yıldız Chalet Museum; Map p110; ☎0212-327 2626; www.millisaraylar.gov.tr), built as a hunting lodge for Sultan Abdül Hamit II in 1880. The şale (chalet) was closed to the public at the time of research, but is well worth visiting if it reopens. (Yıldız Parkı; Çırağan Caddesi, Yıldız; 🚌Çırağan)

Çırağan Palace PALACE

4 ◉ Map p110, C3

Not satisfied with the architectural exertions of his predecessor at Dolmabahçe Palace, Sultan Abdül Aziz (r 1861–76) built his own grand residence at Çırağan, only 1.5km away. Here, architect Nikoğos Balyan, who had also worked on Dolmabahçe, created an interesting building melding European neoclassical with Ottoman and Moorish styles. The Çırağan Palace Kempinski Hotel (p113) now occupies part of the palace. (Çırağan Sarayı; Çırağan Caddesi 84, Ortaköy; 🚌Çırağan)

Eating

Vogue INTERNATIONAL €€€

5 🍴 Map p110, A3

This sophisticated bar-restaurant in a Beşiktaş office block opened in 1997, and feels like it has been going strong since Atatürk was lodging in the nearby Dolmabahçe Palace. A menu of pasta, seafood, sushi, lamb shanks and roast duck, the panoramic Bosphorus views and its various molecular cocktails make Vogue a favourite haunt of the Nişantaşı powerbroker set. (☎0212-227 4404; www.voguerestaurant. com; 13th fl, A Blok, BJK Plaza, Spor Caddesi 92, Akaretler, Beşiktaş; starters ₺26-50, mains ₺30-75; ☺noon-2am; 🍷; 🚌Akaretler)

Banyan ASIAN €€€

6 🍴 Map p110, D2

The menu here travels around Asia, featuring Thai, Japanese, Indian, Vietnamese and Chinese dishes, and including soups, sushi, satays and salads. Banyan claims to serve food for the soul, and you can enjoy it with exceptional views of the Ortaköy Mosque and Bosphorus Bridge, or linger over a sunset cocktail (₺60) at the open-fronted terrace bar. (☎0212-259 9060; www.banyanrestaurant.com; 2nd fl, Salhane Sokak 3, Ortaköy; sushi ₺40, mains ₺80; ☺noon-midnight; 🍷; 🚌Kabataş Lisesi)

Saat Kule Cafe
CAFE €

7 🍽 Map p110, A4

If the onslaught of late Ottoman decadence at Dolmabahçe Palace makes you feel faint, head to its Clock Tower Cafe to recover over a drink or snack. The wraparound windows overlook the Bosphorus, and prices are reasonable for a museum cafe (çay ₺2.50; cappuccino ₺7). (Dolmabahçe Caddesi, Beşiktaş; tost ₺5, mains ₺10; ⏰8.30am-10pm; 🚉Kabataş)

Drinking

Çırağan Palace Kempinski Hotel
BAR

8 🍷 Map p110, C3

Nursing a mega-pricey çay (₺18), coffee (₺20) or beer (₺20) at one of the Çırağan's terrace tables and watching the scene around İstanbul's best swimming pool, which is right on the Bosphorus, lets you sample the lifestyle of the city's rich and famous. The hotel occupies part of the 19th-century Çırağan Palace (p112); look out for the photos of celebrity guests. (📞0212-326 4646; www.kempinski.com; Çırağan Caddesi 32, Beşiktaş; 🚉Çırağan)

Malta Köşkü
CAFE

9 🍷 Map p110, C1

Built in 1870, this unlicensed restaurant and function centre was where Sultan Abdül Hamit II imprisoned his brother Murat V, having deposed him in 1876. The terrace has Bosphorus views, as does the upstairs dining room with its ornate ceiling and chandelier. Food is available, but we recommend sticking to tea or coffee, as the service can be slow and unfriendly. (📞0216-413 9253; www.beltur.istanbul/malta-kosku.asp; Yıldız Parkı; çay ₺2.50, mains ₺20-30; 🚉Çırağan)

Reina
CLUB

10 🍷 Map p110, E2

Gazing up at the Bosphorus Bridge from the waterfront, Reina claims it is 'a meeting point for international statesmen, a location where businesspeople sign agreements worth billions of dollars and where world stars enjoy their meals'. In reality, it's where İstanbul's C-list celebrities congregate, its nouveaux riches flock and where an occasional tourist gets past the doorperson to ogle the spectacle. (📞0212-259 5919; www.reina.com.tr; Muallim Naci Caddesi 44, Ortaköy; ⏰7pm-5am; 🚉Ortaköy)

Sortie
CLUB

11 🍷 Map p110, E1

Behind its high walls, Sortie has long vied for the title of reigning queen of the Golden Mile, nipping at the heels of its rival dowager Reina. It pulls in the city's glamour pusses and poseurs, all of whom are on the lookout for the odd celebrity guest. Its six restaurants open in summer give extra reasons to sortie. (📞0212-327 8585; www.sortie.com.tr; Muallim Naci Caddesi 54, Kuruçeşme; ⏰7pm-late; 🚉Şifa Yurdu)

Top Sights
The Bosphorus

Getting There

🚢 **Ferry** Short tours (₺12, 90 minutes) and full-day tours (one way/return ₺15/25; six hours; 10.35am) depart Eminönü daily.

This mighty strait runs from the Galata Bridge 32km north to the Black Sea (Karadeniz). Over the centuries it has been crossed by conquering armies, intrepid merchants, fishers and many an adventurous spirit. To follow in their wake, hop aboard a ferry cruise. Along the way, you'll see magnificent *yalıs* (waterside timber mansions), ornate Ottoman palaces and massive stone fortresses that line the Asian and European shores (to your right and left, respectively, as you sail down the strait).

Rumeli Hisarı (p116)

Dolmabahçe & Çırağan Palaces

As the ferry starts its journey from Eminönü, look for the 18th-century tower of **Kız Kulesi** (adult/student ₺20/10; ⊙9am-6.45pm; ⚲Üsküdar, ⛔Üsküdar) on a tiny island just off the Asian shore. Just before Beşiktaş, on the European shore, you'll pass grandiose Dolmabahçe Palace (p106). After a brief stop at Beşiktaş, the ferry passes ornate Çırağan Palace (p112), which is now a luxury hotel.

Yalıs

Both sides of the Bosphorus shore are lined with *yalıs* (timber waterside mansions) built by Ottoman aristocracy and foreign ambassadors in the 17th, 18th and 19th centuries. They are now the most prestigious addresses in town, owned by industrialists, bankers and media tycoons.

Ortaköy Mosque

The dome and two minarets of this 19th-century mosque (p109) on the European shore are dwarfed by the adjacent Bosphorus Bridge, which was opened in 1973 on the 50th anniversary of the founding of the Turkish Republic and given a new name (Martyrs of July 15 Bridge) after the events of July 2016.

Beylerbeyi Palace

This 26-room baroque-style **palace** (Beylerbeyi Sarayı; ☎0212-327 2626; www.millisaraylar.gov.tr; Abdullah Ağa Caddesi, Beylerbeyi; adult/student/child under 7yr ₺20/₺5/free; ⊙9am-4.30pm Tue, Wed & Fri-Sun Apr-Oct, to 3.30pm Nov-Mar; ⛴15 from Üsküdar) on the Asian shore was built for Abdül Aziz I. Look for its whimsical marble bathing pavilions; one was for men, the other for the women of the harem.

Bebek

This upmarket suburb is known for its fashion boutiques and chic cafes. As the ferry passes, look for the art nouveau **Egyptian consulate** (Bebek;

☑ Top Tips

▶ The full-day tour involves a three-hour stop in the tourist-trap village of Anadolu Kavağı. Instead, buy a one-way ticket and return on bus 15A, stopping at Kanlıca to visit Hıdiv Kasrı and then transferring to bus 15 for Üsküdar via Küçüksu Kasrı and Beylerbeyi Palace. For timetables see www.iett.gov.tr/en.

▶ If you're keen to visit Ottoman heritage, hop-on, hop-off ferry services depart from Beşiktaş every afternoon (₺15) stopping at Küçüksu Kasrı and Beylerbeyi Sarayı. For timetables see www.denturavrasya.com.

✕ Take a Break

There's a glamorous restaurant with a panoramic terrace in the Sakıp Sabancı Museum (p116), and both Hıdiv Kasrı (p116) and Beylerbeyi Palace (p115) have garden cafes.

🚃22 & 25E from Kabataş, 22RE & 40 from Beşiktaş, 40, 40T & 42T from Taksim) building with its mansard roof.

Küçüksu Kasrı

This ornate **hunting lodge** (🕿0216-332 3303; Küçüksu Caddesi, Küçüksu; adult/student/child under 7yr ₺5/1/free; ⏰9am-4.30pm Tue, Wed & Fri-Sun Apr-Oct, to 3.30pm Nov-Mar; 🚃15, 15E, 15H, 15KÇ, 15M, 15N, 15P, 15ŞN, 15T, 15U from Üsküdar, 14R & 15YK from Kadıköy, ⛴Kabataş) on the Asian shore was built for Sultan Abdül Mecit in 1856–7. Earlier sultans used wooden kiosks here, but architect Nikoğos Balyan designed a rococo gem in marble for his monarch.

Rumeli Hisarı

Just before the Fatih Sultan Mehmet Bridge is majestic **Rumeli Hisarı** (Fortress of Europe; 🕿0212-263 5305; Yahya Kemal Caddesi 42, Rumeli Hisarı; ₺10; ⏰9am-noon & 12.30-4pm Thu-Tue; 🚃22 & 25E from Kabataş, 22RE & 40 from Beşiktaş, 40, 40T & 42T from Taksim), built by order of Mehmet the Conqueror in preparation for his siege of Byzantine Constantinople. For its location, he chose the narrowest point of the Bosphorus, opposite Anadolu Hisarı (Fortress of Asia), which Sultan Beyazıt I had built in 1391.

The Haunted Mansion

On the European shore, look for an eccentric-looking turreted building. Known locally as the Perili Köşk (Haunted Mansion), its construction began in 1910 but was halted during WWI and didn't resume for 80 years,

at which time it was converted into the **Borusan Contemporary** (🕿0212-393 5200; www.borusancontemporary.com; Perili Köşk, Baltalimanı Hisar Caddesi 5, Rumeli Hisarı; adult/student/child under 12yr ₺10/5/free; ⏰10am-8pm Sat & Sun; 🚃22 & 25E from Kabataş, 22RE & 40 from Beşiktaş, 40, 40T & 42T from Taksim) cultural centre.

Hıdiv Kasrı

High on a promontory above Kanlıca, the ferry's second stop, is this gorgeous art nouveau **garden villa** (Khedive's Villa; www.beltur.com.tr; Çubuklu Yolu 32, Çubuklu; admission free; ⏰9am-10pm; ⛴Kanlıca), built by the last Khedive of Egypt as a summer residence for his family.

Emirgan

On the opposite shore is the wealthy suburb of Emirgan, home to the impressive **Sakıp Sabancı Museum** (🕿0212-277 2200; www.sakipsabancimuzesi.org; Sakıp Sabancı Caddesi 42, Emirgan; adult/student/child under 14yr ₺20/10/free, Wed free; ⏰10am-5.30pm Tue, Thu & Fri-Sun, to 7.30pm Wed; 🚃22 & 25E from Kabataş, 22RE & 40 from Beşiktaş, 40, 40T & 42T from Taksim), which hosts international travelling art exhibitions.

Anadolu Kavağı

Passing under the recently built Yavuz Sultan Selim Bridge, the ferry stops at Sarıyer and then crosses to the opposite shore to complete its journey at this former fishing village, which now has a main square full of mediocre fish restaurants.

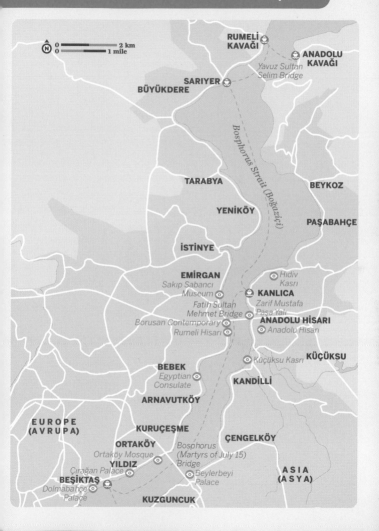

The Best of
İstanbul

Spice Bazaar (p70)
IDEALISTOCK/GETTY IMAGES ©

Best Walks
Sultanahmet

🏃 The Walk

Despite spending the majority of their time in or around Sultanahmet, most visitors see little of this historic district other than their hotel and the major monuments. This walk will take you off the well-worn tourist routes and introduce some lesser-known Ottoman and Byzantine sights.

Start Aya Sofya Meydanı; 🚃 Sultanahmet

Finish Arasta Bazaar; 🚃 Sultanahmet

Length 2.3km; two hours

✕ Take a Break

There are plenty of tea and coffee options in this area, but few are as atmospheric as the Caferağa Medresesi Çay Bahçesi (p56), set in the tranquil courtyard of the historic *medrese* (seminary) of the same name.

Aya Sofya (p24)

❶ Aya Sofya Tombs

Start the walk at Aya Sofya Meydanı (Aya Sofya Sq), turning left into Babıhümayun Caddesi to visit these splendid Ottoman tombs (p34), the final resting places of five sultans.

❷ Fountain of Sultan Ahmet III

This exquisite rococo-style fountain kiosk (1728, p45) outside Topkapı Palace once dispensed cold drinks of water and *şerbet* (sweet cordial) to thirsty travellers.

❸ Soğukçeşme Sokak

Veer down this picturesque street (p52), which is home to re-created Ottoman timber houses and a restored Byzantine cistern.

❹ Caferağa Medresesi

Turn left into Caferiye Sokak to visit this lovely little medrese (p53) (seminary) tucked away in the shadows of Aya Sofya. Commissioned by Süleyman the Magnificent's chief black eunuch, it was built in

1560 and is now home to an organisation supporting traditional handicrafts.

⑤ Sokollu Şehit Mehmet Paşa Mosque

Head towards busy Alemdar Caddesi and then veer left to reach the Hippodrome (p33). Walk its length and then into Şehit Mehmet Paşa Yokuşu. Continue down Katip Sinan Cami Sokak until you reach this splendid Ottoman-era mosque, which has an interior adorned with fine İznik tiles.

⑥ Little Aya Sofya

Veer left down Şehit Çeşmesi Sokak, then turn left into Kadırga Limanı Caddesi and you'll soon arrive at Küçük Ayasofya Caddesi, home to Little Aya Sofya (p34#), one of the most beautiful Byzantine buildings in the city.

⑦ Sphendone

Walk east along Küçük Ayasofya Caddesi and continue left up the hill at Aksakal Caddesi. At the crest is the only remaining built section of the Hippodrome, the

Sphendone). Opposite is a huge carpet shop called Nakkaş (p35) that has a restored Byzantine cistern in its basement.

⑧ Arasta Bazaar

Continue along Nakilbent Sokak, then veer right down Şifa Hamamı Sokak, turning left into Küçük Ayasofya Caddesi and continuing straight ahead to the Arasta Bazaar, a historic row of shops once part of the Blue Mosque *külliye* (mosque complex).

Best Walks
Ottoman Heartland

🏃 The Walk

In the Ottoman era, the narrow streets surrounding the Süleymaniye Mosque were full of timber mansions built by wealthy merchants, high-ranking soldiers and court dignitaries. This walk will take you onto their home turf, passing historically significant building stock that is slowly being restored as part of the Süleymaniye Urban Regeneration Project.

Start Süleymaniye Mosque; 🚊Laleli-Üniversite

Finish Women's Bazaar; Ⓜ Vezneciler

Length 2km; two hours

🍴 Take a Break

Locals swear by the energising properties of *boza*, a viscous drink made from water, sugar and fermented barley, and they head to historic Vefa Bozacısı (p76) for regular fixes during the cooler months.

Şehzade Mehmet Mosque (p70)

❶ Tiryaki Çarşısı

Start in the street fronting the Süleymaniye Mosque (p64). This was once known as the 'Street of the Addicts' due to its preponderance of tea houses selling opium, but is now home to *fasülyes* (bean restaurants) popular with students at nearby İstanbul University and worshippers from the mosque.

❷ Kayserili Ahmet Paşa Konağı

Head down narrow Ayşekadın Hamamı Sokak (opposite the main gate to the mosque) and you will come to this pretty three-storey mansion, once home to a minister of the Ottoman navy and now headquarters of the city's Directorate of Inspection of Conservation Implementation.

❸ Ekmekçizade Ahmetpaşa Medresesi

Continue along Kayserili Ahmetpaşa Sokak and then veer right, passing a football pitch, until you come to this *medrese*, built between 1603 and 1617 by the son of a baker from Edirne who rose up the ranks of Ottoman society to became a *defterder* (first lord of the treasury).

4 Şehzade Mehmet Mosque

From the *medrese*, turn right into Cemal Yener Tosyalı Caddesi and then left into Şehzade Camii Sokak. Pass under the stone arch to reach the rear gate of this elegant mosque (p70), built by order of Süleyman the Magnificent as a memorial to his son, Mehmet, who died of smallpox in 1543.

5 Fatih Anıt Park

After the mosque, head west; you'll see remnants of the majestic Byzantine Aqueduct of Valens (p71) to your right. Cross busy Atatürk Bulvarı and then head towards the aqueduct through this park. The huge *anıt* (monument) in the middle of the park shows Mehment the Conqueror (Fatih) astride his horse.

6 Fatih İtfaiye

On the western edge of Fatih Anıt Park is this handsome Ottoman Revivalist building, which was designed by Greek architect Konstantinos Kiriakidis and built in 1924 as the offices of the local *itfaiye* (fire brigade). Kiriakidis also designed the neighbouring building with its colourful tited facade.

7 Women's Bazaar

Continue through the aqueduct arch and into the Women's Bazaar (Kadınlar Pazarı; p71) on İtfaiye Caddesi, a vibrant local local shopping precinct where there are a number of excellent eateries.

Best Walks
Galata Galivant

🏃 The Walk

The ancient and highly atmospheric neighbourhood of Galata has a very different feel to the rest of the city, perhaps due to its history as a sequestered settlement built and heavily fortified by Genoese traders in the 14th century. These days, boutiques, cafes and art galleries occupy the ground floors of the handsome 19th-century apartment buildings lining the narrow streets running between Galatasaray Meydanı and Galata Meydanı, and then down the hill to Karaköy.

Start Galatasaray Meydanı (Sq); Ⓜ Taksim, Şişhane

Finish Perşembe Pazarı; 🚋 Karaköy

Length 1.4km; two hours

🍴 Take a Break

The streets around the Galata Tower are crammed with cafes; head to the Federal Coffee Company (p97) or Old Java (p99) to enjoy an expertly made coffee.

Camondo Stairs

❶ Galatasaray Meydanı

Start at Galatasaray Lycée, a prestigious public school established in 1868 by Sultan Abdül Aziz, it educates the sons of İstanbul's elite.

❷ Christ Church

From İstiklal Caddesi, head down steep Kumbaracı Yokuşu and into the first street on your right. Walk up the hill to find this Gothic-style Anglican church, dedicated in 1868 as the Crimean Memorial Church and renamed after major restoration in the mid-1990s.

❸ Serdar-ı Ekrem Caddesi

One of the city's most attractive enclaves, this street is home to boutiques, cafes and one of İstanbul's most desired residential addresses, the historic Doğan Apartments. Home to artists, writers, celebrities and expats, this 1895 complex has a beautiful central garden and a handsome entrance featuring stained-glass panels.

❹ Galata Tower

The focal point of the neighbourhood is this

cylindrical tower (p93) constructed by the Genoese in 1348. The tallest structure in the city for centuries, it's still one of İstanbul's most distinctive landmarks.

❺ Camondo Stairs

These sculptural stairs on Tersane Caddesi were commissioned and paid for by the banking family of the same name, and connect Galata with Bankalar Caddesi in Karaköy.

❻ SALT Galata

A cutting-edge cultural centre (p93), SALT aims to be a centre of learning in the city and hosts regular conferences, lectures and workshops. The building also houses a small Ottoman Bank Museum.

❼ Arab Mosque

Built by the Genoese in 1337, this fortresslike building) was the largest of İstanbul's Latin churches. Converted to a mosque after the Turkish conquest of İstanbul (the Conquest), it was given to the recently arrived community of Spanish Muslims after their expulsion from

Spain in the late 15th century.

❽ Perşembe Pazarı

Its name means 'Thursday Market', but the dilapidated area between Tersane Caddesi and the Golden Horn is filled

with tradespeople and shoppers on every day of the week except Sunday. A careful search will unveil crumbling Ottoman *hans* (caravanserais) among the stores selling building and plumbing supplies.

Best
Food

In İstanbul, meals are events to be celebrated. There's an eating option for every budget, predilection and occasion – all made memorable by the use of fresh seasonal ingredients and a local expertise in grilling meat and fish that has been honed over centuries. When you eat out here, you're sure to finish your meal replete and satisfied.

EFESENKO/SHUTTERSTOCK ©

Traditional Eateries

Popular venues for lunch, which is often eaten out, include *lokantas* (eateries serving ready-made food), *pidecis* (Turkish pizza parlours), *kebapçıs* (kebap restaurants) and *köftecis* (meatball restaurants). When not eating dinner at home, locals flock to *meyhanes* (taverns), where an array of hot and cold mezes (tapas-like dishes) are served. Fresh fish is enjoyed in *balık restorans* (fish restaurants) and meat in *ocakbaşıs* (kebap restaurants where the meat is cooked over coals in front of diners).

Contemporary Cuisine

İstanbul has an ever-growing number of eateries serving modern Turkish cuisine. Many of these showcase food by chefs who draw inspiration from Turkey's diverse regional cuisines but do so with a European sensibility.

Street Food

Street vendors pound pavements across İstanbul, pushing carts laden with artfully arranged snacks. Look out for *simits* (sesame-encrusted bread rings), cooked *mısır* (corn on the cob), roasted *kestane* (chestnuts) and *midye dolma* (stuffed mussels). The most famous street snack of all is the *balık ekmek* (fish sandwich).

☑ **Top Tips**

▶ Popular restaurants are busy on Thursday, Friday and Saturday nights. Book ahead.

▶ Restaurant staff don't always speak English – ask staff at your hotel to make your booking.

▶ Alcohol is served in most restaurants reviewed in this book. Exceptions are noted.

Kebap

Best Kebaps

Zübeyir Ocakbaşı Succulent meats cooked over coals. (p95)

Antiochia Sensational southeastern *şiş et* (grilled lamb; p94)

Hamdi Restaurant Panoramic views and Urfa-style kebaps. (p72)

Siirt Şeref Büryan Kebap Recipes from the southeastern city of Siirt. (p73)

Best *Lokantas*

Hayvore Specialising in Black Sea cuisine. (p95)

Erol Lokantası A warm welcome and tasty Turkish cooking. (p37)

Sefa Restaurant Popular workers' eatery near the Grand Bazaar. (p55)

Helvetia Lokanta Vegetarian-friendly hipster hangout. (p96)

Best *Meyhanes*

Eleos Colourful herb-laden mezes and super-fresh fish. (p94)

Karaköy Lokantası Stylish surrounds, bustling vibe and excellent mezes. (p95)

Best Ottoman Palace Cuisine

Asitane Decadent dishes once served to the sultans. (p81)

Deraliye Palace cuisine served in the heart of Sultanahmet. (p35)

Best Sweets

Develi Baklava Tiny place near the Spice Market with a huge (and well-deserved) reputation. (p67)

Karaköy Güllüoğlu The perfect baklava stop at any time of day. (p95)

İnci Pastanesi Famous for its profiteroles. (p96)

Best
Drinking

İstanbul may be the biggest city in a predominantly Muslim country, but let us assure you that İstanbullus like nothing more than a drink or two. To join them, head to the bars and taverns found in Beyoğlu and along the Bosphorus. On the Historical Peninsula, the drinks of choice are çay (tea) or *Türk kahve* (Turkish coffee).

ALI962/SHUTTERSTOCK ©

Rakı

Turkey's most beloved tipple is rakı, a grape spirit infused with aniseed. Similar to ouzo, it's served in long thin glasses and is drunk neat or with water, which turns the clear liquid chalky white.

Turkish Wine

Turkey grows and bottles its own *şarap* (wine), which has greatly improved during the past decade but is expensive due to high government taxes. If you want red wine, ask for *kırmızı şarap*; for white, *beyaz şarap*. Most Turkish winemakers use local varietals including *boğazkere* and *buzbağ* (strong-bodied reds), *emir* (a light and floral white), *kalecik karası* (an elegant red) and *narince* (a fruity yet dry white).

Turkish Coffee

A thick and powerful brew, *Türk kahve* (Turkish coffee) is drunk in a couple of short sips. If you order a cup, you will be asked how sweet you like it – *çok şekerli* means 'very sweet', *orta şekerli* 'middling', *az şekerli* 'slightly sweet' and *şekersiz* or *sade* 'not at all'.

Turkish Tea

Drinking çay is the national pastime. Sugar cubes are the only accompaniment and you'll find these are needed to counter the effects of long brewing; otherwise, try asking for it *açık* (weaker).

☑ **Top Tips**

▶ Though you shouldn't drink the grounds in the bottom of your cup of *Türk kahve*, you may want to read your fortune in them – check the Turkish Coffee/Fortune Telling section of the website of İstanbul's longest-established purveyor of coffee, **Kurukahveci Mehmet Efendi** (www.mehmetefendi.com) for a guide.

Busy street in Taksim

Best Rooftop Bars & Cafes

Mikla Spectacular views and a stylish clientele. (p97)

360 The city's most famous bar, for good reason. (p98)

A'YA Rooftop Lounge Amazing sunset views over Sultanahmet. (p39)

Mimar Sinan Teras Cafe Student hangout with panoramic water views. (p76)

Best Street-Level Bars & Cafes

Unter In the midst of the hipster enclave of Karaköy. (p98)

Geyik Fashionable venue on Cihangir's Akarsu Yokuşu. (p98)

Alex's Place Asmalımescit speakeasy popular with the bohemian set. (p98)

Solera Huge choice of Turkish wine by the glass. (p99)

Best Coffee

Federal Coffee Company Popular neighbourhood cafe and roastery. (p97)

Manda Batmaz Traditional coffee house in Beyoğlu. (p98)

Kronotrop Speciality coffee bar in Cihangir. (p88)

Karabatak Julius Meinl coffee and a laid-back vibe. (p99)

Best
Architecture

İstanbul is one of the world's great architectural time capsules. Locals still live within city walls built by Byzantine emperors, worship in Ottoman-era mosques and reside in grand 19th-century apartment buildings.

Byzantine Architecture

The city spent 1123 years as a Christian metropolis and structures including aqueducts, cisterns and public squares survive from this era. After the Conquest, many churches were converted into mosques; despite the minarets, you can usually tell a church-cum-mosque by its distinctive red bricks.

Ottoman Architecture

After the Conquest, sultans wasted no time putting their architectural stamp on the city, constructing mosques, palaces, hamams, *medreses* (theological schools) and *yalıs* (waterside timber mansions). The best of these buildings were commissioned by Süleyman the Magnificent and designed by his court architect, Mimar Sinan. Later sultans focused their attention on palaces and hunting lodges featuring ornate external detail and ostentatious interior decoration; these and other buildings of the era have been collectively dubbed 'Turkish baroque'.

Ottoman Revivalism & Modernism

In the late 19th century, architects created a blend of European architecture alongside Turkish baroque, with some concessions to classic Ottoman style. This style has been dubbed 'Ottoman Revivalism' or First National Architecture. When the 20th century arrived and Atatürk proclaimed Ankara the capital of the republic, İstanbul lost much of its investment capital – as a result, few notable buildings date from this period.

☑ **Top Tips**

▶ Architectural walking tours of the city are conducted by **İstanbul Walks** (www.istanbulwalks.com), a company run by a group of history, conservation and architecture buffs. Tours run daily and can be booked at short notice.

Basilica Cistern (p30)

Best Byzantine Buildings

Aya Sofya One of the world's great buildings, with a magnificent interior. (p24)

Little Aya Sofya Exquisite church building now functioning as a mosque. (p34)

Basilica Cistern Extraordinary engineering and a magnificent symmetrical design. (p30)

Best Ottoman Buildings

Topkapı Palace Pavilion-style architecture and a gorgeous landscaped setting. (p44)

Süleymaniye Mosque The greatest of the city's imperial mosques, with many intact outbuildings. (p64)

Blue Mosque A profusion of minarets, domes and fine İznik tilework. (p28)

Kılıç Ali Paşa Hamamı Gorgeous hamam commissioned by an Ottoman admiral. (p132)

Best Turkish Baroque Buildings

Dolmabahçe Palace Imposing exterior and over-the-top interior decoration. (p106)

Beylerbeyi Palace Imperial splendour on the Asian shore of the Bosphorus. (p115)

Çırağan Palace Little sister to Dolmabahçe, possessing plenty of Ottoman opulence. (p112)

Best Contemporary Adaptive Reuse

SALT Galata A 1892 bank building cleverly converted into gallery, library and restaurant spaces. (p93)

Beyazıt State Library Magnificent renovation of the Beyazıt Mosque's 19th-century *imaret* (soup kitchen; p71).

İstanbul Modern A shipping warehouse converted into a huge contemporary art gallery. (p92)

Sakıp Sabancı Museum Sympathetic modern additions to one of the largest mansions on the Bosphorus. (p116)

Best
Hamams

Succumbing to a soapy scrub in a steamy hamam is one of İstanbul's quintessential experiences. Not everyone feels comfortable with baring all (or most) of their body in public, though. If you include yourself in this group, a number of the city's spas offer private hamam treatments.

IZZET KERIBAR/GETTY IMAGES ©

Bath Procedure

Upon entry you will be shown to a *camekan* (entrance hall), allocated a dressing cubicle and given a *peştemal* (bath wrap) and plastic sandals. Undress and put these on. Females may keep their knickers on or wear a bikini bottom, although this is optional. Males usually just wear the *peştemal* (but always leave it on). You'll then be shown to the *hararet* (steam room), where you can sit on the side or lie on top of the central *göbektaşı* (heated raised platform). A traditional Turkish bath experience involves having an attendant wash, scrub and massage you. Soap, shampoo and towel are included in these treatments; you may wish to bring your own *kese* (exfoliating mitten).

Ayasofya Hürrem Sultan Hamamı (☎0212-517 3535; www.ayasofyahamami. com; Aya Sofya Meydanı 2; bath treatments €85-170, massages €40-75; ⊗8am-10pm; 🚋Sultanahmet) A meticulously restored twin hamam dating from 1556, and offering one the most luxurious traditional bath experiences in the Old City.

Kılıç Ali Paşa Hamamı (☎0212-393 8010; http:// kilicalipasahamami. com; Hamam Sokak 1, off Kemeraltı Caddesi, Tophane; traditional hamam ritual ₺170; ⊗women 8am-4pm, men 4.30-11.30pm; 🚋Tophane) This hamam's interior is simply stunning and the

place is run with total professionalism.

Çemberlitaş Hamamı (☎0212-522 7974; www. cemberlitashamami. com; Vezir Han Caddesi 8, Çemberlitaş; self-service ₺70, bath, scrub & soap massage ₺115; ⊗6am-midnight; 🚋Çemberlitaş) This twin hamam was designed by the great architect Sinan and is among the most beautiful in the city.

Four Seasons İstanbul at the Bosphorus (☎0212-381 4000; www.fourseasons.com/ bosphorus; Çırağan Caddesi 28, Beşiktaş; 30/45/60min hamam experience €125/155/185; ⊗9am-9pm; 🚋Bahçeşehir Ünv. or Çırağan) The gorgeous marble hamam is perfect if you're looking for an indulgent Turkish bath experience.

Best
Çay Bahçesis

İstanbullus have perfected the art of *keyif* (quiet relaxation), and practise it at every possible opportunity. *Çay bahçesis* (tea gardens) are *keyif* central, offering their patrons pockets of tranquility off the noisy and crowded streets. Games of *tavla* (backgammon), glasses of tea, nargiles (water pipes) and quiet conversations are usually the only distractions on offer.

ROSSHELEN/SHUTTERSTOCK ©

Erenler Nargile ve Çay Bahçesi Set in the vine-covered courtyard of the Çorlulu Ali Paşa Medrese near the Grand Bazaar. (p76)

Lale Bahçesi Located in a sunken courtyard in the shadow of the Süleymaniye Mosque. (p76)

Derviş Aile Çay Bahçesi Leafy retreat with spectacular Blue Mosque view. (p38)

Hazzo Pulo Pasajı Atmospheric cobbled courtyard off İstiklal Caddesi. (p85)

Cafe Meşale Occasional live music and a mixed crowd behind the Blue Mosque. (p39)

Caferağa Medresesi Çay Bahçesi Tranquil hideaway near Aya Sofya; no nargiles. (p56)

☑ Top Tips

▶ If ordering a nargile (pictured), you'll need to specify what type of tobacco you would like. Most people opt for *elma* (with tobacco that has been soaked in apple juice, giving it a sweet flavour and scent). A nargile will cost between ₺20 and ₺25 and can be shared (you'll be given individual plastic mouthpieces).

Best
Museums &
Galleries

İstanbul has always embraced art and culture. In Byzantine times, the emperors amassed huge collections of antiquities, importing precious items from every corner of their empire. The Ottoman sultans followed the same tradition, building extraordinary imperial collections. And these days the country's big banks and business dynasties vie to outdo each other in building and endowing galleries and cultural centres.

MELINERD/SHUTTERSTOCK ©

Best Museums

İstanbul Archaeology Museums An extraordinary collection of antiquities, classical sculpture, historical artefacts and Ottoman tilework. (p48)

Museum of Turkish & Islamic Arts World-class collection of Oriental carpets and calligraphy. (p33)

Museum of Great Palace Mosaics Showcases a stunning mosaic pavement dating from Byzantine times. (p34)

Museum of Innocence Orhan Pamuk's nostalgic museum/conceptual art project. (p92)

Carpet Museum A showcase of Anatolian carpets housed in three galleries in an 18th-century *imaret* (soup kitchen; p51).

İstanbul Naval Museum Home to a spectacular collection of imperial *caïques* (ornately decorated wooden rowboats). (p111)

Best Galleries

Pera Museum Turkey's most significant collection of Orientalist paintings. (p86)

İstanbul Modern Spotlights 20th-century Turkish painting alongside high-profile international artists. (p92)

ARTER Four floors of cutting-edge contemporary art on İstiklal Caddesi. (p85)

Sakıp Sabancı Museum Hosts top-notch travelling international art exhibitions. (p116)

National Palaces Painting Museum Nineteenth-century Turkish paintings from the Dolmabahçe Palace collection. (p107)

☑ **Top Tips**

▶ If you plan to visit the major museums and monuments, the **Museum Pass İstanbul** (http://www.muze.gov.tr/en/museum-card) will save you money and time.

Best
Views

Studded with historic minarets, domes and towers, the İstanbul skyline is the city's greatest asset. The hilly topography is fringed with waterways (the Bosphorus, Golden Horn and Sea of Marmara) and retains a surprisingly generous allocation of green spaces, including heavily treed parks and garden cemeteries. Together, these attributes offer views that are guaranteed to delight.

GAVIN HELLIER/ROBERTHARDING/GETTY IMAGES ©

Scenic Viewpoints

The city's many hills are invariably crowned with Ottoman mosques, most of which incorporate scenic terraces. And these weren't the only Ottoman buildings that were designed to make the most of their location – imperial palaces and pleasure kiosks were almost always sited to take advantage of spectacular water vistas.

Rooftop Bars & Cafes

In İstanbul one of the most delightful experiences on offer is to enjoy a drink or meal in a rooftop cafe, bar or restaurant. Occupying the top floors of hotels and commercial buildings in Sultanahmet, Beyoğlu

and along the Bosphorus shore, these venues give the city's eating and drinking scenes a unique allure.

Best Restaurant, Cafes & Bar Views

Mikla Spectacular 360-degree views across the city. (p97)

Hamdi Restaurant Panoramic views of the Old City, Golden Horn and Bosphorus. (p72)

360 Across the Bosphorus to the Old City and Asian shore. (p98)

Mimar Sinan Teras Cafe Views of the Golden Horn and Bosphorus from the terrace. (p76)

Cihannüma One of the best views in the Old City. (p39)

A'YA Rooftop Lounge The vista includes Aya Sofya and the Bosphorus. (p39)

CUE İstiklal Enjoy the Bosphorus and Old City view while dancing the night away. (p98)

Best Views from Monuments

Topkapı Palace Marble Terrace and Konyalı Restaurant Terrace. (p44)

Rumeli Hisarı Extraordinary Bosphorus views from the ramparts. (p116)

Dolmabahçe Palace The Bosphorus location ensures spectacular views. (p106)

Süleymaniye Mosque Golden Horn vistas from the terrace behind the mosque. (p64)

Best
Shopping

İstanbullus have perfected the practice of shopping, and most visitors are quick to follow their lead. Historic bazaars, colourful street markets and an ever-expanding portfolio of modern shopping malls cater to every desire and make sourcing a souvenir or two both easy and satisfying.

Bathwares

Attractive towels, *peştemals* (bath wraps) and bathrobes made on hand looms are sold in designer bathwares shops around the city. Other popular purchases include hamam bowls and olive-oil soaps.

Carpets & Kilims

The carpet industry is rife with commissions, fakes and dodgy merchandise, so you need to be extremely wary in all of your negotiations and dealings.

Textiles

Turkey's southeast is known for its textiles, and there are examples aplenty on show in the Grand Bazaar. Also look for pashminas (the real things, not cheap synthetic imitations) and decorative tribal textiles that have made their way here from Central Asia.

Ceramics

Many of the tiles you see in the tourist shops have been painted using a silk-screen printing method and this is why they're cheap. Hand-painted bowls, plates and other pieces are more expensive.

Jewellery

Look for work by the city's growing number of artisans creating contemporary pieces inspired by local culture.

☑ **Top Tips**

▶ *Lokum* (Turkish delight; pictured) makes a great present for those at home. It's sold in speciality shops around the city.

Best Homewares

Hiç Designer homewares made by local and international artisans. (p101)

Özlem Tuna Artisanally designed and made homewares and jewellery. (p57)

Hamm Stylish showcase of contemporary Turkish furniture and lighting. (p102)

NYKS Elegantly packaged olive-oil candles. (p101)

ALP AKSOY/SHUTTERSTOCK ©

Colourful ceramics

İznik Classics Hand-painted collector-item Turkish ceramics. (p40)

Best Bath Wares

Jennifer's Hamam Towels, robes and wraps produced on old-style shuttled looms. (p39)

Abdulla Natural Products Olive-oil soaps, cotton towels and a large range of *peştemals* (bath wraps; p77).

Derviş Soaps, towels and wraps to beautify your bathroom. (p77)

Eyüp Sabri Tuncer Well-priced colognes, soaps and lotions. (p102)

Best Jewellery

Necef Antik & Gold Byzantine- and Ottoman-inspired pieces in the Grand Bazaar. (p77)

Ümit Berksoy Artisan jeweller based in the Grand Bazaar. (p78)

Best Textiles

Yazmacı Necdet Danış Richly hued bolts of fabric and a range of scarves. (p78)

Mekhann Hand-woven silk from Uzbekistan, plus a range of finely woven shawls. (p78)

Mehmet Çetinkaya Gallery Antique pieces in the Arasta Bazaar. (p40)

Cocoon Striking textiles, rugs and handicrafts from Central Asia. (p40)

Best *Lokum*

Altan Şekerleme Selling cheap and delicious *lokum* since 1865. (p77)

Ali Muhiddin Hacı Bekir Family-run business established in the city more than two centuries ago. (p57)

Hafız Mustafa An İstanbul institution, with branches across the Old City. (p56)

Best Handicrafts

Nahıl Felting, lacework, embroidery and all-natural soaps made by economically disadvantaged women in Turkey's rural areas. (p100)

Khaftan Calligraphy, ceramics, Ottoman prints and contemporary paintings. (p40)

Artrium Antique ceramics, calligraphy, maps, prints and jewellery. (p102)

Best
Nightlife

MARK HORN/GETTY IMAGES ©

There's a nightlife option for everyone in İstanbul. You can dance the night away in a glamorous nightclub on the Bosphorus, listen to jazz in a dimly lit Beyoğlu basement, cram into a crowded live-music venue or drink rakı and burst into song at a cheap and rowdy *meyhane* (tavern).

Clubs

The best nightclubs are in Beyoğlu and on the 'Golden Mile' between Ortaköy and Kuruçeşme on the Bosphorus. Friday and Saturday are the busiest nights of the week and action rarely kicks off before 1am. Note that many of the Beyoğlu clubs close over summer, when clubbing action moves to the Black Sea or Aegean coasts.

Live-Music Venues

Beyoğlu is the heart of the city's live-music scene. Locals have a particular fondness for jazz, which is performed at dedicated clubs and festivals.

Meyhanes

On weekends locals like to get together with friends and family at *meyhanes*. Some *meyhanes* focus solely on food, but others host small groups of musicians who move from table to table playing *fasıl* music, emotion-charged Turkish folk or pop songs played on traditional instruments. These are favourites with large groups, who pay ₺70 to ₺100 to enjoy a generous set menu with either limited or unlimited choices from the bar.

☑ **Top Tips**

▶ If you're keen to visit a Bosphorus club, consider booking to have dinner in its restaurant – otherwise you could be looking for a lucky break or a tip of at least ₺100 to get past the door staff .

▶ When İstanbullus go out clubbing they dress to kill. You'll need to do the same to get past the door staff at the Bosphorus clubs or into the rooftop bar-clubs in Beyoğlu.

Reina (p113)

Best Live-Music Venues

Babylon Bomonti The city's most famous live-music venue.

Nardis Jazz Club Beloved of true aficionados. (p100)

Salon Strong on jazz, but also hosts alternative, experimental and world music. (p100)

Best Clubs

Indigo Four-floor electronic-music temple. (p99)

CUE İstiklal Cocktails and dancing high above Beyoğlu. (p98)

Reina Queen of the Golden Mile superclubs. (p113)

Worth a Trip

İstanbul's pre-eminent live-music venue, **Babylon Bomonti** (☎0212-334 0190; www.babylon.com.tr; Tarihi Bomonti Bira Fabrikası, Birahane Sokak 1, Bomonti; admission free; Ⓜ Osmanbey) occupies an atmospheric former beer factory in an up-market arts enclave close to the Osmanbey metro stop in Nişantaşı and is a regular haunt of the city's bohemian set. In summer, action moves to the club's beach clubs in the Black Sea resort of Kilyos and in Çeşme on the Aegean coast.

Best
For Kids

LENISECALLEJA PHOTOGRAPHY/SHUTTERSTOCK ©

İstanbul is a great destination for a family-friendly break. Children might whinge about the number of mosques and museums on the itinerary, but they'll be appeased by the fantastic baklava, *lokum* (Turkish Delight) and *dondurma* (ice cream) on offer, as well as the castles, underground cisterns and parks waiting to be explored.

Best for Toddlers

Gülhane Park Playground equipment and plenty of open space. (p52)

Hippodrome Loads of open space to run around in. (p33)

Best for Bigger Kids

Grand Bazaar Scavenger Hunt Forget shopping, exploring the Grand Bazaar on a scavenger hunt offered by Alternative City Tours is much more fun. (p61)

Bosphorus Cruise Spot monuments from both sides of the boat. (p114)

Rumeli Hisarı Kids love castles! Just be careful that junior knights and princesses don't go too close to the edge on the battlements. (p116)

Basilica Cistern It's creepy (way cool), and kids can explore the walkways suspended over the water. (p30)

Mado Turkish ice cream. Yum. (p109)

Best for Teenagers

İstanbul Modern Plenty of exhibits – including lots of multimedia – that will amuse and engage. (p92)

Cooking Courses Some teenagers see the kitchen as offering more than a refrigerator just waiting to be raided. (p142)

☑ **Top Tips**

▶ Children under 12 receive free or discounted entry to most museums and monuments.

▶ Children under seven travel free on public transport.

▶ Most footpaths are cobbled, so strollers aren't very useful.

Best
For Free

FILIP FUXA/SHUTTERSTOCK ©

The backpackers who flocked to İstanbul in the 1960s and '70s would blow their meagre budgets if they headed this way today. Fortunately, the ever-increasing price of hotel rooms, transport and meals is counterbalanced by an array of free top sights that can be visited. These include parks, museums, churches, mosques and tombs.

Best Mosques & Tombs

Süleymaniye Mosque The grandest and most beautiful of the city's mosques. (p64)

Rüstem Paşa Mosque Tile-adorned gem hidden in the Bazaar District. (p67)

Aya Sofya Tombs Ottoman tiles, calligraphy and decorative paintwork. (p34)

Blue Mosque Curvaceous exterior and huge tiled interior. (p28; pictured)

Tomb of Sultan Ahmet I Decorated with fine 17th-century İznik tiles. (p34)

Best Parks & Gardens

Gülhane Park Popular for picnics and promenading, with some great views. (p52)

Hippodrome Ancient chariot arena decorated with obelisks, columns and a fountain. (p33)

Yıldız Park Huge leafy retreat by the Bosphorus shore. (p112)

Hıdıv Kasrı Pretty art nouveau villa in a formal garden. (p116)

Best Galleries & Museums

ARTER One of the most prestigious art venues in town, with an international exhibition program. (p85)

Hünkar Kâsrı Tile-adorned pavilion attached to the New Mosque. (p70)

SALT Galata Cultural centre with library and exhibition spaces. (p93)

Pera Museum Free admission every Friday between 6pm and 10pm; Wednesdays also free for students. (p86)

Sakıp Sabancı Museum Free entry on Wednesday. (p116)

Best Bazaars & Markets

Grand Bazaar One of the world's oldest and most atmospheric shopping malls. (p60)

Spice Bazaar Join the crowds at this ancient marketplace near the Eminönü docks. (p70)

Fish Market Beyoğlu's historic produce market sells much more than *balık* (fish; p85).

Women's Bazaar Fresh produce market in Fatih where local *kadınlar* (women) do their daily shop. (p71)

Best
Culinary Courses & Tours

İstanbul Eats (http://istanbuleats.com; tours per person US$75-125) Full-day culinary walks around the Old City, Bazaar District, Beyoğlu, Kadıköy and the Bosphorus, as well as evenings spent sampling kebaps in Aksaray's 'Little Syria' district or visiting *meyhanes* (Turkish taverns) in Beyoğlu. All are conducted by the dedicated foodies who produce the excellent blog of the same name.

Turkish Flavours (☎0532 218 0653; www.turkishflavours.com; tours per person US$80-125) Offers walks and cooking classes, including a five-hour ' Market Tour' that starts at Eminönü's Spice Bazaar and then goes to Kadıköy by ferry, where it tours the produce market and finishes with a lavish lunch at Çiya Sofrası. Other tours include a 'Meyhane Experience' and a vegetarian food tour through Karaköy and Kadıköy.

Cooking Alaturka (☎0212-458 5919; www.cookingalaturka.com; Akbıyık Caddesi 72a, Cankurtaran; classes per person incl meal €65; ⏱10.30am & 4.30pm by reservation Mon-Sat; 🚇Sultanahmet) This culinary school is cooking up a storm under its Turkish-Italian ownership. Suitable for both novices and experienced cooks, its convivial 2½-hour classes give a great introduction to Turkish cuisine, from classic meze to Ottoman dishes such as Circassian chicken.

İstanbul on Food (☎0538 966 7671; http://istanbulonfood.com; tour US$100) New to the city's food-tour scene, this small outfit offers a popular four-hour 'Twilight at Taksim' tour, where you'll wander through the side streets on either side of İstiklal Caddesi sampling plenty of street food and kebaps before popping into a *meyhane* for a rakı and finishing with baklava at Karaköy Güllüoğlu.

Urban Adventures (☎0532 641 2822; www.urbanadventures.com; tours adult €27-82, child €22-79) This professional outfit runs a number of cultural tours including a 3½-hour night tasting walk in Beyoğlu and a dinnertime visit to Small Projects İstanbul, an NGO working to support Syrian refugees in the city.

İstanbul Walks (☎0554 335 6622, 0212-516 6300; www.istanbulwalks.com; 1st fl, Şifa Hamamı Sokak 1; tours adult €35-75, child under 2/7yr free/30% discount; 🚇Sultanahmet) Specialising in cultural tourism, this company is run by history buffs and offers a range of guided tours conducted by knowledgeable English-speaking guides. Tours concentrate on İstanbul's various neighbourhoods, but there are also tours of major monuments, a Turkish coffee trail, and a Bosphorus and Golden Horn cruise by private boat.

Survival Guide

Survival Guide

Before You Go

When to Go

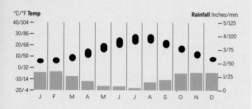

°C/°F Temp
40/104 —
30/86 —
20/68 —
10/50 —
0/32 —
-10/14 —
-20/-4 —

Rainfall Inches/mm
— 5/125
— 4/100
— 3/75
— 2/50
— 1/25
— 0

J F M A M J J A S O N D

➡ **Spring (Mar–May)**
Possibly the best time of the year to visit; tulips bloom in April.

➡ **Summer (Jun–Aug)**
The heat can seem un-relenting, but shoulder-season hotel rates and the İstanbul Music Festival compensate.

➡ **Autumn (Sep–Nov)**
A lovely time of year, with gentle breezes and a profusion of cultural festivals.

➡ **Winter (Dec–Feb)**
Winters are often bone-chillingly cold. Low-season rates apply in hotels except over the Christmas–New Year period.

Book Your Stay

➡ Staying in Sultanahmet makes sense if you plan to spend your time visiting museums and the bazaars.

➡ Beyoğlu is a better op-tion for those interested in eating, drinking and clubbing.

➡ Book your room as far in advance as possible, particularly if you are visiting during the high season (Easter–May, September–October and Christmas–New Year).

➡ Many hotels offer a dis-count of between 5% and 10% for cash payments.

➡ Room rates in the low season (November–Easter, excluding Christ-mas to New Year) and shoulder season (June to August) are often discounted.

➡ A Value-Added Tax (VAT) of 8% is added to all hotel bills; it's usually included in the price quoted when you book.

➡ Many hotels provide a free airport transfer from Atatürk International Airport if you stay three nights or more.

➡ Breakfast is almost always included in the room rate.

➡ For writers' recommendations and online booking check Lonely Planet's website: www.lonelyplanet.com.

Best Budget

Louis Appartements (www.louis.com.tr/galata) Keenly priced and well-equipped suites and rooms near Galata Tower.

Marmara Guesthouse (www.marmaraguesthouse. com) Friendly, family-run budget pension in the heart of Sultanahmet.

Hotel Alp Guesthouse (www.alpguesthouse.com) Attractive rooms and a wonderful roof terrace with sea views.

Best Midrange

Hotel Ibrahim Pasha (www.ibrahimpasha.com) Chic contemporary style with Ottoman overtones; overlooks the Blue Mosque.

Karaköy Rooms (www. karakoyrooms.com) Hip location, decor and vibe.

Hotel Empress Zoe (www. emzoe.com) Atmospheric boutique choice near Aya Sofya perfectly balancing charm and comfort.

TomTom Suites (www. tomtomsuites.com) Elegant suites and a rooftop restaurant with spectacular views.

Sirkeci Mansion (www. sirkecimansion.com) Wonderful family choice with impressive service, entertainment program and facilities.

Witt Istanbul Hotel (www. wittistanbul.com) Huge, super-stylish suites and a rooftop garden.

Vault Karaköy (www. thehousehotel.com) Stylish and evocative meld of old and new in a grand bank building.

Best Top End

Four Seasons Istanbul at the Bosphorus (www. fourseasons.com/bosphorus) Restaurants, impressive spa, luxe rooms and spectacular pool.

Pera Palace Hotel (www. perapalace.com) Exceptional levels of service and comfort in historic surrounds.

Best Self-Catering Options

Istanbul Place Apartments (www.istanbulplace. com/) Stylish and well-set-up apartments in the Galata district.

Casa di Bava (www.casa dibavaistanbul.com) Suite hotel with an arty vibe and well-equipped apartments and rooms.

Money-Saving Tips

➡ If you plan to visit three or more museums, purchase a Museum Pass İstanbul (p152).

➡ The İstanbulkart (p147) offers a considerable discount on public-transport fares (₺2.20 to ₺2.45 according to the destination, as opposed to the usual ₺4, with additional transfers within a two-hour journey window – ₺1.75 for the first transfer, ₺1.60 for the second and ₺1.40 for all subsequent transfers).

➡ Check whether your hotel offers free airport pick-ups and drop-offs.

Manzara Istanbul (www.manzara-istanbul.com) Locations across Beyoğlu.

Hamamhane (www.hammamhane.com) Self-catering rooms in a vibrant local neighbourhood.

Arriving in İstanbul

☑ **Top Tip** For the best way to get to your accommodation, see p17.

➡ There are currently two international airports in the city, both of which are operating at or close to capacity. This has prompted the Turkish Government to announce construction of a new, much larger, airport 50km north of the city centre. The first stage of the new airport's construction is due to be completed by 2018 but the facility won't be fully operational until 2025.

Atatürk International Airport

➡ **Atatürk International Airport** (IST, Atatürk Havalimanı; ☎+90 444 9828; www.ataturkairport.com) is 23km west of Sultanahmet; the *dış hatlar* (international terminal) and *iç hatlar* (domestic terminal) are side by side.

➡ A taxi costs around ₺45 from the airport to Sultanahmet, ₺55 to Taksim Meydanı (Sq).

➡ An efficient metro service (₺4) travels between the airport and Yenikapı, from where you can take another metro (₺4) to Şişhane and Taksim in Beyoğlu. For Sultanahmet, alight from the first metro at Zeytinburnu, from where it's easy to connect with the tram (₺4) travelling to Kabataş via Sultanahmet and Eminönü. The metro station is on the lower ground floor beneath the international departures hall – follow the 'Metro/Subway' signs down the escalators and through the underground walkway. Services depart every two to 10 minutes or so from 6am to midnight.

➡ If you're staying near Taksim Meydanı, take the Havataş Airport Bus (₺11). This travels between the arrivals hall and Cumhuriyet Caddesi, next to Taksim Meydanı, every 30 minutes between 4am and 1am; the trip takes between 40 minutes and one hour depending on traffic.

Sabiha Gökçen International Airport

➡ **Sabiha Gökçen International Airport** (SAW, Sabiha Gökçen Havalimanı; ☎0216-588 8888; www.sgairport.com) is 50km east of Sultanahmet, on the Asian side of the city.

➡ A taxi costs around ₺155 from the airport to Sultanahmet, ₺140 to Beyoğlu.

➡ The Havataş Airport Bus (₺14) travels from the airport to Taksim Meydanı between 3.30am and 1am. The trip takes approximately 90 minutes. If you're heading towards the Old City, you'll then need to take the funicular (₺4) to Kabataş and the tram (₺4) from Kabataş. There's also a Havataş service to Kadıköy (₺9, 4.15am to 12.45am), from where you can take a ferry (₺4) to Eminönü, Karaköy or Beşiktaş.

Getting Around

Tram

☑ **Best for...** Travelling between Sultanahmet and Beyoğlu.

➡ An excellent *tramvay* (tramway) service runs from Bağcılar, in the city's west, to Zeytinburnu (where it connects with the metro from the airport) and on to Sultanahmet and Eminönü. It then crosses the Galata Bridge to Karaköy (to connect with the Tünel) and Kabataş (to connect with the funicular to Taksim Meydanı). A second service runs from Cevizlibağ, closer to Sultanahmet on the same line, through to Kabataş.

➡ Services run every five minutes from 6am to midnight.

➡ The fare is ₺4; *jetons* (ticket tokens) are available from machines at every tram stop and İstanbulkarts can be used.

Funicular

☑ **Best for...** The steep climb uphill from the tram stops to İstiklal Caddesi.

➡ A funicular called the Tünel carries passengers between Karaköy, at the base of the Galata Bridge (Galata Köprüsü), to Tünel Meydanı, at one end of İstiklal Caddesi. The service operates every five minutes between 7am and 10.45pm and a *jeton* (travel token) costs ₺4.

➡ A second funicular carries passengers from Kabataş, at the end of the tramline, to Taksim Meydanı, where it connects to the metro. The service operates every five minutes from 6am to midnight and a *jeton* costs ₺4.

Metro

☑ **Best for...** Trips to the airport.

➡ The M1A connects Yenikapı, southwest of Sultanahmet, with the airport. This stop at 16 stations along the way.

➡ The M2 connects Yenikapı with Taksim, stopping at three stations along the way: Vezneciler, near the Grand Bazaar; on the new bridge across the Golden Horn (Haliç); and at Şişhane,

İstanbulkart

Rechargeable **İstanbulkart** (www.istanbulkart. iett.gov.tr/en) travel cards can be used on most trams, ferries, buses and metro services, and offer a considerable discount on fares. They can also be used to pay for fares for more than one traveller (one swipe per person per ride).

The cards can be purchased from machines at metro and funicular stations for a nonrefundable charge of ₺10, which includes ₺4 in credit. If you buy yours from a street kiosk near a tram or bus stop, you will usually pay ₺8 (no credit).

İstanbulkarts can be recharged with amounts between ₺5 and ₺150 at kiosks or at machines at ferry docks and metro and bus stations.

Individual *jetons* (ticket tokens) can be purchased from ticket machines or offices at tram stops, *iskeles* (ferry docks) and funicular and metro stations, but it's much cheaper and easier to use an İstanbulkart.

You must have an İstanbulkart to use a bus.

near Tünel Meydanı in Beyoğlu. From Taksim it travels northeast to Hacıosman via nine stations. A branch line, the M6, connects one of these stops, Levent, with Boğaziçi Üniversitesi near the Bosphorus.

➡ The Marmaray line, connects Kazlıçeşme, west of the Old City, with Ayrılık Çeşmesi, on the Asian side. This travels via a tunnel under the Sea of Marmara, stopping at Yenikapı, Sirkeci and Üsküdar en route.

➡ Metro services depart every five minutes between 6am and midnight. *Jetons* (ticket tokens) cost ₺4 and İstanbulkarts can be used. Go to www. istanbul-ulasim.com.tr for maps of the metro network.

Ferry
☑ **Best for...** Sightseeing and travelling on the Bosphorus and Golden Horn (Haliç).

➡ The main ferry docks are at the mouth of the Golden Horn (Eminönü and Karaköy) and at Beşiktaş, a few kilometres northeast of Galata Bridge, near Dolmabahçe Palace. There are also busy docks at Kadıköy

and Üsküdar on the Asian (Anatolian) side. Ferries travel many routes around the city, but the following routes are those commonly used by travellers:

Eminönü–Anadolu Kavağı (Long Bosphorus Tour); one service per day.

Eminönü–Kadıköy Approximately every 15 to 20 minutes from 7.30am to 9.10pm.

Eminönü–Üsküdar Approximately every 20 minutes from 6.50am to 10.30pm.

Karaköy–Kadıköy Approximately every 20 minutes from 6.20am to 11pm.

Üsküdar–Karaköy– Eminönü–Kasımpaşa– Hasköy–Ayvansaray– Sütlüce–Eyüp The Golden Horn (Haliç) ferry; hourly from 7.30am to 7.45pm.

➡ *Jetons* (ticket tokens) cost ₺4 for most trips and it's possible to use İstanbulkarts on all routes except the Bosphorus tours. The main ferry company is **İstanbul Şehir Hatları** (İstanbul City Routes; www. sehirhatlari.com.tr), but

Turyol (www.turyol.com) and **Dentur Avraysa** (www.denturavrasya.com) also offer Bosphorus cruises and services between the European and Asian shores.

Taxi
☑ **Best for...** Travelling at night or if you care short on time.

➡ Taxi rates are very reasonable (from Sultanahmet to Taksim Meydanı will cost around ₺15) and there are no evening surcharges.

➡ Ignore taxi drivers who insist on a fixed rate as these are much higher than you'd pay using the meter.

➡ Note that few of the city's taxis have seatbelts.

➡ If you take a taxi from the European side to the Asian side over one of the Bosphorus bridges, it is your responsibility to cover the toll (₺4.75). The driver will add this to your fare. There is no toll when crossing from Asia to Europe.

Bus
☑ **Best for...** Exploring the Bosphorus villages.

➡ The major *otobus* (bus) stations are at Taksim

Meydanı (underground), Beşiktaş, Eminönü, Kadıköy and Üsküdar.

➡ Most services run between 6am and 11pm.

➡ You must have an İstanbulkart before boarding.

➡ For bus timetables and route details, see the website of the **İstanbul Elektrik Tramvay ve Tünel** (İETT, Istanbul Electricity, Tramway and Tunnel General Management; www.iett.gov.tr).

Essential Information

Business Hours

➡ Opening hours vary wildly across businesses and services in İstanbul. The following is a very general guide.

Bars Afternoon to early morning

Nightclubs 11pm till late

Post Offices & Banks 8.30am to 5pm Monday to Friday

Restaurants & Cafes Breakfast 7.30am to 10.30am, lunch noon

to 2.30pm and dinner 6.30pm to 10pm

Shops 10am to 7pm Monday to Saturday

Electricity

230V/50Hz

Emergency

Ambulance ☑112

Fire ☑110

Police ☑155

Money

➡ The currency is the Türk Lirası (Turkish Lira; ₺).

➡ ATMS are widely available.

➡ Most hotels, car-hire agencies, shops, pharmacies, entertainment

venues and restaurants accept Visa and Master-Card; Amex isn't as widely accepted and Diners is often not accepted. Inexpensive eateries usually accept cash only.

➡ The 24-hour *döviz bürosus* (exchange bureaus) in the arrivals halls of the international airports usually offer competitive rates.

➡ Tip 10% in restaurants and ₺2 per bag for porters; in taxis round up the fare to the nearest ₺1.

Public Holidays

➡ Banks, offices and government services close for the day on the following secular public holidays.

New Year's Day 1 January

National Sovereignty & Children's Day 23 April

Labor & Solidarity Day 1 May

Commemoration of Atatürk, Youth & Sports Day 19 May

Democracy and Freedoms Day 15 July

Victory Day 30 August

Republic Day 29 October

➡ Religious festivals are celebrated according to

Mosque Etiquette

➡ Remove your shoes before walking on the mosque's carpet; you can leave them on shelves near the mosque door or place them in one of the plastic bags provided and carry them with you.

➡ Women should always cover their heads and shoulders with a shawl or scarf; both women and men should dress modestly.

➡ Avoid visiting mosques at prayer times – within 30 minutes of when the *ezan* (call to prayer) sounds from the mosque minaret – and also around Friday lunch, when weekly sermons and group prayers are held.

➡ Speak quietly and don't use the flash on your camera if people are praying.

the Muslim lunar Hejira calendar. Two of these festivals (Şeker Bayramı and Kurban Bayramı) are also public holidays. **Şeker Bayramı** is a three-day festival at the end of Ramazan, and **Kurban Bayramı**, the most important religious holiday of the year, is a four-day festival whose date changes each year. During these festivals, banks and offices are closed and hotels, buses, trains and planes are heavily booked.

➡ Though most restaurants and cafes open to serve non-Muslims during the holy month of Ramazan (called Ramadan in other countries), it's polite to avoid smoking, eating and drinking in the street during this period.

Safe Travel

➡ İstanbul is a generally safe city, but you should employ common sense when exploring. Be particularly careful near the historic city walls, as these harbour vagrants and people with substance-abuse problems – don't walk here alone or after dark.

➡ Single males should be wary if approached by locals and invited to go to a club or bar – this often leads to a shakedown in a local mafia-operated venue.

➡ If a shoeshine person drops their brush in front of you, ignore it – it's a time-tested scam to con you into paying for their services.

➡ Be particularly wary when dealing with carpet sellers – never, ever agree to buy rugs under the assurance that an advantageous resale brokered by the dealer awaits in your home country.

➡ Recently, political tensions within the country and the region have led to terrorist incidents including bomb attacks in areas and facilities frequented by tourists. Visitors should monitor their country's travel advisories and stay alert at all times.

Telephone

Phone Codes

➡ If you are in European İstanbul and wish to call a number in Asian İstanbul, you must dial 📞0216. If you are in Asian İstanbul and wish to call a number in European İstanbul, dial 📞0212. Do not use a prefix (that is, don't use the 🖉0212/6) if you are calling a number on the same shore. Local mobile numbers start with a four-digit code beginning with 🖉05.

Country code 🖉90

Intercity code 🖉0 + local code

International access code 🖉00

Mobile Phones

➡ Mobile phone reception is excellent in İstanbul.

➡ There are three major networks: **Turkcell** (www.turkcell.com.tr), **Vodafone** (www.vodafone.com.tr) and **Avea** (www.avea.com.tr). Each has shops throughout the city selling prepaid SIM cards (*kontürlü SIM karts*) that can be used in foreign phones. The cards operate for up to 120 days and cost around ₺85 (including ₺30 in local calls credit). An internet data pack with the SIM will cost around ₺25/30/40/60 for 1/2/4/8 GB and a pack for international calls will cost an extra ₺30/60 or so for one/two hours' credit. Ask the staff in the shop to suggest the most cost-effective solution for your needs. Once you have the SIM, it can be recharged with *kontürs* in amounts of ₺20 upwards.

➡ When you purchase the SIM, ask the staff to organise the activation for you (you'll need to show your passport). The account should activate almost immediately.

➡ Note that Turkey uses the standard GSM network operating on 900MHz or 1800MHz (so not all US and Canadian phones work here).

Toilets

➡ Most public toilets are of the Western (ie sit-down) variety; those in mosques are exceptions and are mainly squat-style.

➡ Toilets near transport hubs and stations and in and around major sights usually charge a fee of ₺1.

➡ There are handy public toilets in the Grand Bazaar, on the Hippodrome in Sultanahmet and in the underpasses next to the ferry docks at Eminönü and Karaköy.

Tourist Information

➡ The **Ministry of Culture & Tourism** (www.turizm.gov.tr) currently operates three tourist information offices or booths in the city and has booths at both international airports. In our experience, the Sirkeci office is the most helpful and the Sultanahmet office is the least helpful.

Tourist Office – Atatürk International Airport (🖉0212-465 3547; International Arrivals Hall; ⊙9am-9pm)

Tourist Office – Sabiha Gökçen International Airport (🖉0216-588 8794; ⊙8am-7pm)

Tourist Office – Sirkeci Train Station (Map p50; 🖉0555 675 2674, 0212-511 5888; Sirkeci Gar, Ankara Caddesi, Sirkeci; ⊙9.30am-6pm mid-Apr–Sep, 9am-5.30pm Oct–mid-Apr; 🚇Sirkeci)

Tourist Office – Sultanahmet (Map p32; 🖉0212-518 8754; Hippodrome, Sultanahmet; ⊙8.30am-6.30pm mid-Apr–Sep, 9am-5.30pm Oct–mid-Apr; 🚇Sultanahmet)

Tourist Office – Taksim (🖉0212-233 0592; www.kulturturizm.gov.tr; ground fl, Seyran Apartmanı, Mete Caddesi, Taksim; ⊙9.30am-6pm mid-Apr–Sep, 9am-5.30pm Oct–mid-Apr; 🚇Taksim)

Museum Pass İstanbul

Valid for 120 hours (five days) from your first museum entrance, the **Museum Pass İstanbul** (www.muze.gov.tr/en/museum-card) costs ₺85 and allows single entrances to Topkapı Palace and Harem, Aya Sofya, Aya İrini, İstanbul Archaeology Museums, Museum of Turkish and Islamic Arts, Great Palace Mosaics Museum, Kariye Museum (Chora Church), Galata Mevlevi Museum, Fethiye Museum, Rumeli Hisarı, Yıldız Sarayı and İstanbul Museum of the History of Science & Technology in Islam. Purchased individually, admission fees to these sights will cost ₺260, so the pass represents a possible saving of ₺175. It can be purchased from some hotels and from the ticket offices of all of the museums it covers.

Travellers with Disabilities

➡ İstanbul can be challenging for mobility-impaired travellers. Roads are potholed and footpaths are often crooked and cracked.

➡ Government-run museums are free of charge for people with disabilities. Public and private museums and sights that have wheelchair access and accessible toilets include Topkapı Palace, the İstanbul Archaeology Museums, İstanbul Modern, the Pera Museum and the Rahmi M Koç Museum. The last three of these also have limited facilities to assist accessibility for

visitors with impaired vision.

➡ Airlines and most four- and five-star hotels have wheelchair access and at least one room set up for guests with a disability, while all public transport is free for them, and the metro and trams can be accessed by people in wheelchairs.

➡ **FHS Tourism and Event** (www.accessibleturkey.org) is an İstanbul-based travel agency that has a dedicated department organising accessible travel packages and tours.

Visas

At the time of research, nationals of the following countries (among others) could enter Turkey for up to three months with only a valid passport (no visa required): Denmark, Finland, France, Germany, Greece, Israel, Italy, Japan, New Zealand, Sweden and Switzerland. Russians could enter for up to 60 days.

Nationals of the following countries (among others) needed to obtain an electronic visa (www.evisa.gov.tr) before their visit: Australia, Canada, China, Ireland, Mexico, Netherlands, Norway, Portugal, Spain, Taiwan, UK and USA. These visas were valid for between 30 and 90 days and for either a single entry or a multiple entry, depending on the nationality. Visa fees cost US$25 to US$70, depending on nationality.

Indian nationals needed to 'meet certain conditions' before being granted an electronic visa.

Your passport must have at least six months' validity remaining, or you may not be admitted into Turkey. See the website of the **Ministry of Foreign Affairs** (www.mfa.gov.tr) for the latest information.

Language

Pronouncing Turkish is pretty simple for English speakers as most Turkish sounds are also found in English. If you read our pronunciation guides as if they were English, you should be understood just fine. Note that the symbol **ew** represents the sound 'e' pronounced with rounded lips (as in 'few'), and that the symbol **uh** is pronounced like the 'a' in 'ago'. The Turkish **r** is always rolled and **v** is pronounced a little softer than in English. Word stress is quite light in Turkish – in our pronunciation guides the stressed syllables are in italics.

To enhance your trip with a phrasebook, visit **lonelyplanet.com**. Lonely Planet iPhone phrasebooks are available through the Apple App store.

Basics

Hello.
Merhaba.   mer·ha·ba

Goodbye. (when leaving)
Hoşçakal.   hosh·cha·kal

Goodbye. (when staying)
Güle güle.   gew·le gew·le

Yes.
Evet.   e·vet

No.
Hayır.   ha·yuhr

Please.
Lütfen.   lewt·fen

Thank you.
Teşekkür   te·shek·kewr
ederim.   e·de·reem

Excuse me.
Bakar mısınız.   ba·kar muh·suh·nuhz

Sorry.
Özür dilerim.   er·zewr dee·le·reem

How are you?
Nasılsınız?   na·suhl·suh·nuhz

Fine, and you?
İyiyim, ya siz?   ee·yee·yeem ya seez

Do you speak English?
İngilizce   een·gee·leez·je
konuşuyor   ko·noo·shoo·yor
musunuz?   moo·soo·nooz

I don't understand.
Anlamıyorum.   an·la·muh·yo·room

Eating & Drinking

The menu, please.
Menüyü   me·new·yew
istiyorum.   ees·tee·yo·room

What would you recommend?
Ne tavsiye   ne tav·see·ye
edersiniz?   e·der·see·neez

I don't eat (meat).
(Et) yemiyorum.   (et) ye·mee·yo·room

I'd like (a/the) ...
... istiyorum.   ... ees·tee·yo·room

a (cup of) coffee
bir (fincan) kahve   beer (feen·jan) kah·ve

a (jug of) beer
bir (fıçı) bira   beer (fuh·chuh) bee·ra

Enjoy your meal.
Afiyet olsun.   a·fee·yet ol·soon

Cheers!
Şerefe!   she·re·fe

That was delicious!
Nefisti!   ne·fees·tee

The bill, please.
Hesap lütfen.   he·sap lewt·fen

Shopping

I'd like to buy ...
... almak | al·mak
istiyorum. | ees·tee·yo·room

I'm just looking.
Sadece | sa·de·je
bakıyorum. | ba·kuh·yo·room

How much is it?
Ne kadar? | ne ka·dar

It's too expensive.
Bu çok pahalı. | boo chok pa·ha·luh

Do you have something cheaper?
Daha ucuz | da·ha oo·jooz
birşey var mı? | beer·shay var muh

Emergencies

Help!
İmdat! | eem·dat

Call a doctor!
Doktor çağırın! | dok·tor cha·uh·ruhn

Call the police!
Polis çağırın! | po·lees cha·uh·ruhn

I'm lost.
Kayboldum. | kai·bol·doom

I'm ill.
Hastayım. | has·ta·yuhm

Where's the toilet?
Tuvalet nerede? | too·va·let ne·re·de

Time & Numbers

What time is it?
Saat kaç? | sa·at kach

It's (10) o'clock.
Saat (on). | sa·at (on)

in the morning
öğleden evvel | er·le·den ev·vel

in the afternoon
öğleden sonra | er·le·den son·ra

in the evening
akşam | ak·sham

now
şimdi | sheem·dee

yesterday	dün	dewn
today	bugün	boo·gewn
tomorrow	yarın	ya·ruhn

1	bir	beer
2	iki	ee·kee
3	üç	ewch
4	dört	dert
5	beş	besh
6	altı	al·tuh
7	yedi	ye·dee
8	sekiz	se·keez
9	dokuz	do·kooz
10	on	on

Transport & Directions

Where is the (market)?
(Pazar yeri) | (pa·zar ye·ree)
nerede? | ne·re·de

What's the address?
Adresi nedir? | ad·re·see ne·deer

Can you show me (on the map)?
Bana (haritada) | ba·na (ha·ree·ta·da)
gösterebilir | gers·te·re·bee·leer
misin? | mee·seen

Please put the meter on.
Lütfen | lewt·fen
taksimetreyi | tak·see·met·re·yee
çalıştırın. | cha·luhsh·tuh·ruhn

I'd like a ticket to ...
... bir bilet | ... beer bee·let
lütfen. | lewt·fen

Does it stop at ...?
... durur mu? | ... doo·roor moo

I'd like to get off at ...
... inmek | ... een·mek
istiyorum. | ees·tee·yo·room

Behr the Scenes

Send Us Your Feedback

We love to hear from travellers – your comments help make our books better. We read every word, and we guarantee that your feedback goes straight to the authors. Visit **lonelyplanet.com/contact** to submit your updates and suggestions.

Note: We may edit, reproduce and incorporate your comments in Lonely Planet products such as guidebooks, websites and digital products, so let us know if you don't want your comments reproduced or your name acknowledged. For a copy of our privacy policy visit lonelyplanet.com/privacy.

Acknowledgements

Cover photograph: Grand Bazaar, Guido Cozzi/4Corners ©

Photograph pp4-5: Blue Mosque, Tim Gerard Barker/Getty Images ©

Virginia's Thanks

Many thanks to Pat Yale, Mehmet Umur, Emel Güntaş, Faruk Boyacı, Atilla Tuna, Görgün Taner, Tahir Karabaş, Jen Hartin, Eveline Zoutendijk, George Grundy, Ann Nevans, Tina Nevans, Jennifer Gaudet, Özlem Tuna, Monica Fritz, Leon Yildirimer, Luca Fritz, Teoman Göral, Meltem İnce Okvuran, Nurullah Çınar, Deniz Ova, Zeynep Unanç, Antony Doucet, Sabiha Apaydın, Saliha Yavuz and the many others who shared their knowledge and love of the city with me.

This Book

This 6th edition of Lonely Planet's *Pocket İstanbul* guidebook was researched and written by Virginia Maxwell. The previous edition was also written by Virginia. This guidebook was produced by the following:

Destination Editors Lorna Parkes, Tom Stainer, Clifton Wilkinson
Product Editors Grace Dobell, Amanda Williamson
Senior Cartographer Corey Hutchison
Book Designer Clara Monitto

Assisting Editor Janice Bird
Cover Researcher Naomi Parker

Thanks to Emma Åsenius, Imogen Bannister, Kate Chapman, Liz Heynes, Andi Jones, Sumi Prasad, Kirsten Rawlings, Allison Schell, Tony Wheeler

Index

See also separate subindexes for:
Eating p158
Drinking p159
Entertainment p159
Shopping p159

Sights 000
Map Pages **000**

Our Writer

Virginia Maxwell

Although based in Australia, Virginia spends part of each year in Turkey. As well as working on the previous five editions of this Pocket guide, she also writes Lonely Planet's *İstanbul* city guide, covers İstanbul, İzmir and the North Aegean for the *Turkey* guide, and writes about the city for a host of international magazines and websites.

Published by Lonely Planet Global Limited
CRN 554153
6th edition – February 2017
ISBN 978 1 78657 234 9
© Lonely Planet 2017   Photographs © as indicated 2017
10 9 8 7 6 5 4 3 2 1
Printed in China